LEARNING CALIFORNIA HISTORY

LEARNING CALIFORNIA HISTORY

Essential Skills for the Survey Course and Beyond

Gordon Morris Bakken
California State University, Fullerton

Brenda Farrington
Santa Ana College

Harlan Davidson, Inc. • Wheeling, Illinois 60090-6000

Developmental editor/copy editor: Andrew J. Davidson
Production editor/text designer: Lucy Herz
Proofreader: Katie Heider
Printer: BookCrafters, Inc.
Cover photographs courtesy of Wayne Engstrom,
        Placentia, California.
Cover design: DePinto Graphic Design

Manufactured in the United States of America
03 02 01 00 99 1 2 3 4 5 BC

TO THE MEMORY OF WARREN A. BECK
COLLEAGUE, MENTOR, FRIEND

Contents

Acknowledgements

First we must thank Andrew Davidson, who suggested we write this book. He had the vision to see the need for a different type of learning and assessment instrument, and he tenaciously guided the book to publication. We also must thank Linda Gaio-Davidson for all her support and encouragement in the process.

In developing this book, we contracted a huge debt of gratitude to Angela Henderson, director of tutorial services at Mount San Antonio College, and David Rhone, Saddleback High School's premier advance placement teacher in American history and chair of the Social Studies Department, for many hours spent reading the manuscript and for helpful suggestions for revision. We likewise are indebted to the students of California history who worked through the exercises and critiqued them while this work was still a product of a copying machine—at least they got class credit for their labor.

Finally, and perhaps most important, for their help in conducting research for this book, we thank the dedicated professional employees of the California Section of the California State Library in Sacramento, The Huntington Library, The Bancroft Library, and the California State University–Fullerton Library. We Californians are most fortunate to have so many able and dedicated librarians and archivists working to preserve and portray our state's past.

Gordon Morris Bakken   Brenda Farrington
California State University–Fullerton   Santa Ana College

A Note to Instructors: Students Welcome!

Having taught California history for many years, we believe a course in the social sciences should enhance basic skills, enrich general education, facilitate career preparation, and stimulate personal growth and development. Toward that end, we present *Learning California History.*

Much more than a supplementary textbook on California history or politics, this book has been designed as a dynamic and thought-provoking workbook to compliment any of the standard survey textbooks on California history currently available. In *Learning California History,* our objective is twofold: first, to survey the writing of California history and introduce students to basic social science research methods, providing historical thinking materials to promote reading, research, and writing skills; second, to offer practical student-assessment tools certain to help instructors as well as students.

We recognize that most students enrolled in California history and politics courses are not history or political science majors and have no firm grounding in the analytical skills expected of those who are. But we affirm that strong methodological and theoretical knowledge coupled with strong communications skills are essential for anyone seeking employment in today's competitive job market. Students must learn to think critically, research exhaustively, and express analytically the products of their efforts.

That said, students need concrete things to think about, research, and express. The exercises in this book are grounded in primary sources; after reading selected passages from primary-source documents produced contemporaneously with the events they portray, students are asked to "interrogate" them, to extrapolate meaning in the context of each document's time. We also ask students to determine how some of the ideas contained in those documents influenced California politics.

Based on our teaching experience and the pilot-testing of this book with students at the community-college and university levels, we acknowledge that the ability of students differs widely and that there is no single method of appraising performance. We admit that the best assessment methods usually consume more time: instructors must read more student work and students must spend more time in analytical thought—as opposed merely to memorizing material temporarily in order to regurgitate it later for an exam or in a paper. Probably the best way to determine which parts of this book will work best for your students is to employ an educated trial-and-error method. Regardless of which portions of this book you choose to employ, throughout its focus remains on enhancing student knowledge and skills. As you probably have already surmised, *Learning California History* does not offer traditional tests for the assessment of student performance. Rather, this book contains exercises that help build the student's knowledge of California history and politics, even as the completion of those exercises hones the student's ability to think critically and communicate effectively.

The Texts

In each chapter, contextual, methodological, research, or interpretive subjects receive brief treatment. Chapter One considers the textbook writers of the past and present. Students must understand that every history is contingent upon the perspective of its author. California's textbook writers were products of their times, and this is reflected in their work. (In the case of this book, your authors are the products of classroom experience in California garnered over the last three decades.) Chapter Two explains the teaching and learning functions of historians and invites students to participate in the venture through active, hands-on exercises. Chapter Three introduces the reader to critical thinking and emphasizes its importance in historical research. Chapter Four presents context for analysis. Here students discover that historical analysis of causation is not a formula, not an equation: it is far more difficult and requires an appreciation of all the surrounding circumstances viewed through the widest possible lens. Chapter Five takes that wide-angle snapshot of historical events and breaks it down to discover its component parts. Chapter Six proposes to decode interpretation in historical literature, often the most difficult undertaking facing students of history as well as professional historians. Hopefully, this book will impress upon all who read it that even after all of the facts are gathered, they must be interpreted to find meaning. Chapter Seven puts students into the library, the local historical society, and online to find primary and secondary sources. Chapter Eight poses provocative questions while suggesting numerous research topics that pertain to twentieth-century events, inviting students to bring all of the skills learned in the previous chapters together in the creation of an interpretive research paper.

The Exercises

In the book's first exercise, in Chapter Two, we ask students to "interrogate" a newspaper story about a gunfight. All are cautioned to read the text for what it represents, as well as for what it actually communicates and why. Instructors may wish to use responses to this exercise as an assessment of each student's skill level. Alternatively, each question in the exercise can serve as a topic for classroom discussion. Further, the research questions the exercise poses may lead to reading in suggested secondary sources, useful in elaborating on and interpreting the meaning of the event in question. Finally, some professors may find this exercise useful as a basis for oral examinations; such face-to-face interrogative dialogue allows substantial, in-depth evaluation.

Chapter Three has three exercises. The first involves the California Constitutional Convention of 1849. Whether one is studying history, politics, or government, the 1849 California Constitution is a foundational document, and the debates of the convention delegates reveal a good deal about the times, the issues, and the politics of constitution-making. Students of California history also will learn to see the event and the document in a national context. The words of the delegates are provocative, and, again, this exercise affords a common documentary field for classroom discussion or individual student assessment. The second exercise asks students to ponder an editorial decrying the operation of so-called "secret societies," in this case the Grange. In the third exercise students will consider a document that reveals changing male and female expectations of marriage at the turn of the century.

The exercise in Chapter Four forces analysis of context and research in secondary sources to arrive at an informed evaluation. This exercise holds out a higher level of document interrogation and assessment. Critical thinking skills are clearly necessary for the task, but students must go beyond the text to tease out the meaning of the document. Some instructors may find role-playing useful here, with students taking the positions of some of the delegates and arguing their respective policy positions.

The documents presented in the Chapter Five exercise are topical. Among other things, these sources should help students appreciate the problems women faced in obtaining even their basic civil rights. And while California's women were part of a national struggle for rights, they had a political context different from that of many other American women. The questions in this exercise are increasingly difficult and call upon students to use their research skills more intensely. Some professors may find the exercise useful for classroom research assessment, which, in this case, requires all students to read all thirteen documents and answer the questions based on those materials. Then, individual students or collaborative research groups are asked to read selected or all secondary sources listed in the chapter. The recommended secondary sources afford students a foundation for comparison with the primary-source documents they have just encountered. One thing students may wish to explore is the difference between the primary and secondary sources in terms of objectivity.

Chapter Six includes a discussion of cliometrics. Accordingly, this chapter's exercises provide crime statistics and ask students to interpret the numbers. Students will quickly learn that numbers have little meaning out of context and without analytic connections to the real world. Here students are asked to discern how statistics can better be used to promote interpretation. Instructors may find this section useful in explaining research design as well as in explaining history's links to economics and political science.

Chapter Seven is filled with documents about crime and justice in California in the second half of the nineteenth century. Readers are certain to realize that these documents raise issues that resonate today. After ample opportunity to practice their skills in citation and research note taking, students will go on to design their own research projects to determine how the political system responds to issues that show no sign of fading away.

Chapter Eight has several exercises concerning Rose E. Bird, a Chief Justice of the California Supreme Court. Here, the issues of crime and the death penalty are evident. Students are asked to assess critically the veracity of sources, explore the nature of modern politics, and determine the societal impact of an institution. We hope that rather than merely questioning documents, students will at this point move on to researching the nature of current politics through the lens of the politics of justice. This chapter also contains a variety of exercises about California Progressives, critical elections, and current politics. Some elections we ask students to consider were shaped by critical issues of race and gender, but we present these exercises as alternatives to the first three concerning Rose E. Bird.

Finally, in many of the exercises you will encounter optional exercises and activities that invite the student reader "To Go Deeper." In these places students are directed to more detailed sources on the subject in question. Instructors may want to use "Go Deepers" as extra-credit assignments or as part of a broader research and writing agenda. Hopefully, some readers will be intrigued by the primary sources they encounter herein and will welcome these suggestions for further reading.

Assessment

As indicated above, this book is designed to facilitate classroom discussion and provide students with a practice ground for historical research, interpretation, and writing. The issues raised by the primary-source documents reproduced in the pages that follow, as well as by the secondary sources recommended throughout, provide interpretative windows for students considering California today. As you will see, the exercises in *Learning California History* ask students to write, and write, and write. Some instructors may wish to use this book in parts, as exercises in critical thinking and writing. Some may find that it can be treated as a journal or portfolio to be assessed periodically and turned in at the end of the semester or quarter. Portfolio assessment affords the instructor a longitudinal view of student learning, methodological development, and writing-skills. The results for the students are likely to be meaningful, particularly in terms of diagnostic evaluation and feedback from the instructor. Finally, by concentrating the assessment period at term's end, the portfolio approach circumvents the test anxiety some students experience.

As mentioned, this book suggests a number of research topics. Instructors may wish to assign research papers on any of these topics, allowing students to benefit along the way from the completion of the exercises. Alternatively, instructors may wish to assign research topics to collaborative learning groups. Once collaborative research and writing groups have been formed, periodic conferences between the instructor and the groups are highly useful. During these sessions, instructors can probe the group's progress, suggest fruitful avenues of inquiry, or, perhaps, hint of a motherlode in the documents section of the library or local historical society.

Regardless of how you choose to use this book, we hope students of California history and politics find it evocative, a springboard to future learning, research, and writing.

Writing California History: A History

You may find it interesting to learn that the earliest histories of our state were not written by professional historians. In fact, California was part of the United States for almost a century before professional historians addressed the subject of California history. The same could be said for many states, with serious consideration of state history emerging only after World War II. Nevertheless, today California libraries contain a great number and variety of California histories, and students must be aware that each one bears a unique context and philosophy.[1]

The following review of California history textbook writers is a brief historiographical survey. Historiography is the study of the principles, theory, and history of historical writing to determine the methods, perspectives, or interpretative influences that historians bring to their work. You will quickly note that the subjects of history expand with time, that the interpretations of our state's past change, and that a given author's background, training, and political orientation influence his or her writing. Historians frequently say that history must be rewritten by each succeeding generation. So too our state's textbooks!

John S. Hittell was one of California's first historians. He made his living as a journalist and was historian of the Society of California Pioneers, an organization dedicated to recording and preserving the history of the state's first white settlers. Commissioned for the bicentennial in 1876, his work, *A History of San Francisco and Incidentally of the State of California,* was, as one might expect, clearly celebratory and biographically focused on the pioneers. Further, Hittell's choice to concentrate on San Francisco and its "glorious" past was an expected result of his patrons' wishes. Though no one can deny that Hittell's history was a subjective account, in it he preserved some of the facts of California history in a highly readable format.

Taking up a great deal more space on library shelves today is the work of Hubert Howe Bancroft, a merchant capitalist of California's first quarter century of statehood. Besides making and selling legal forms and law encyclopedias and digests, Bancroft's firm, Bancroft, Whitney and Company of San Francisco, took the official reports and court records (available to the public) and published them in multiple volumes called Reports for sale to the public—mostly lawyers. (Today his company still performs this job for lawyers, but the Bancroft Co. name is in name only.)

Bancroft conducted his business with great vigor, proclaiming in his law books: "The Survival of the Fittest—A Trinity of Reports Selected and Annotated."[2] For

---

1. The best discussion of the early historiography is Gerald D. Nash, "California and Its Historians: An Appraisal of the Histories of the State," *The Pacific Historical Review* 50 (Nov., 1981), pp. 387–413. Unless otherwise indicated in the footnotes, the bulk of this chapter draws on Nash's fine work.
2. Gordon Morris Bakken, *Practicing Law in Frontier California* (Lincoln: University of Nebraska Press, 1991), pp. 30-1.

Bancroft, collecting historical facts was much like collecting cases, and he viewed the writing of history in the same light: as a business for profit. To garner facts for his venture in history, he dispatched a legion of researchers. Bancroft's research team roamed far and wide, mining the archives of the American West, Mexico, and Central America. They scanned old newspapers as well as public records. Some interviewed prominent figures of particular locales. This vast collection of "fact" today resides at the Bancroft Library on the campus of The University of California–Berkeley. Though a perusal of the collection will lead the modern researcher to conclude that the range of Bancroft's inquiry was narrow at best, Bancroft and staff produced a thirty-nine-volume set of "history" that sold profitably to libraries and book collectors.

Seven of Bancroft's thirty-nine volumes speak to California history. Clearly, he had opened a vast new storehouse of information for a public that read and enjoyed history. But how much of California's history had that public actually read? Not much by contemporary comment! Rather, those seven volumes of California history published between 1884 and 1890 comprise mostly stories about California politics. For Bancroft, social, economic, and intellectual issues were seldom worthy of print. Questions about race, class, and gender had not occurred to Bancroft's researchers and were clearly not the stuff of popular consumption. Bancroft had produced more pages of California history than Hittell, but his work, too, portrayed an early impression of politics and sensational events rather than history as we have come to understand it.

Josiah Royce, a native Californian and a first-rank philosopher, produced the first interpretive history of the state, but he limited his inquiry to the initial decade of American control.[3] His work, *California, From the Conquest in 1846 to the Second Vigilance Committee in San Francisco: A Study of American Character,* found print in 1886. Actually focusing on the period 1849 to 1856, Royce asked a philosophical question regarding the values at play between individuals in a rapidly growing community. Here the moral fiber of Californians was tested by the anarchy of the instant city, the chaos of lawlessness, and the consequent search for order.

Royce's work told a great deal about the American character in the caldron of state formation. He found John C. Frémont's actions creating the Bear Flag Republic immoral but considered the nonviolent approach of Thomas O. Larkin worthy of praise. Royce arrived at his conclusions based on his reading of primary documents and an interview he conducted with John Charles and Jessie Benton Frémont in New York in 1884. As Royce's work attests, the Gold Rush was a time of testing during which people exhibited both the best and worst in the American character. Californians put away the animosity over slavery then raging in the rest of the nation to forge a state government. In the sprawling mining camps of the day, women injected family and religious values into male-dominated communities. Yet at the same time people exhibited civic irresponsibility and xenophobia. Conflict too often degenerated into violence. Lynch law or the disrespect for the rule of law indicated that the social fabric was unraveling. Royce knew most of this from his childhood in Grass Valley and from his mother's reminiscences.

Royce's stab at writing history has much to recommend it. First, he relied upon documentation. Second, he took the facts beyond their statement and offered an interpretation. Finally, he sought balance in his work and moved beyond a celebration of the conquest of California by the American pioneers. There was a very

---

3. The best discussion of Royce's work is Robert V. Hine, *Josiah Royce: From Grass Valley to Harvard* (Norman: University of Oklahoma Press, 1992). pp. 146–60.

vulgar side to California's history and the American character, one steeped in violence, acquisitiveness, and fraud. His history related the social condition of ordinary people as well as the "pioneers." Royce recognized the relationships between people and place: the land's splendid scenery as well as the challenges posed by its geography were part of the human experience. Here he sought the collective consciousness of a people within a social order. Royce tried to tease out the changing meaning of the California experience within the traditions of his times. Many of his methods and observations deserve the attention of today's students.

Theodore H. Hittell, John's brother and a successful San Francisco attorney, entered the California history business in 1885 with the first two volumes of his *History of California,* followed in 1897 by the final two volumes. Theodore Hittell viewed California history through the political lens, organizing his narrative around the successive administrations of Spanish, Mexican, and American governors. His work was heavily documented and constitutes a major contribution to California political history, but Hittell was particularly critical of Hispanic rule and its values.

A counterattack followed. Helen Bandini's *History of California* (1908) gloried in the state's Hispanic heritage and romanticized that experience. Another journalist writing history, Bandini wrote for a popular audience, and professional historians gave her work little heed. In his *History of California* (1911) John S. McGroaty took a similar approach. To McGroaty, another journalist, the Spanish mission was the center of civilization and culture, bringing Indians to Christ and meaning to a frontier. Furthermore, his work revealed his unabashed love for the state's scenery and climate. California was, by his lights, the last best place in the country.[4] Gertrude Atherton, a novelist, tried her hand at "history" with *California: An Intimate History* (1914), commingling nostalgia for those arcadian rancho days with progressive reform rhetoric. The book was a tract for a pastoral day long gone, but it was popular with contemporary readers and is fruitfully remembered. Hot on her heels was Zoeth Eldredge's five-volume *History of California* (1915). Eldredge was a banker with time to read Bancroft and Theodore Hittell and to write about the good old days of the Dons and the march of "civilization" to its romantic and selfless conclusion in his lifetime. It should be clear by now that students picking up these volumes today will not find objective criticism in them, much less an account of the ugly underside of the mission or rancho. Racism and patriarchy were hardly topics fit for ink in romantic California.

In the 1920s, with the appearance of works by Charles E. Chapman and Robert Glass Cleland, the nature of California history began to transform. Chapman's *History of California: The Spanish Period* (1921) evolved from his dissertation work under Herbert Eugene Bolton at Berkeley. Chapman's research in archives in Spain and Mexico gave his popular history a professional aura. Cleland's *History of California: The American Period* (1922) finally pushed California history into a national and international context, though most of Cleland's words centered on the period 1846–1860. Cleland and Chapman were trained historians, and they brought the canon of professional historical method to the writing of California history.

Cleland, in particular, resuscitated the state's early heroes and, much like writers before him, kept the pioneers clearly before the reading public. Other works followed. In 1944 he published *From Wilderness to Empire: A History of California, 1542–1900* and in 1947 *California in Our Time.* But Cleland was far more than a conventional history writer, finding in letters, maps, and artifacts other his-

---

4. Today others argue that Montana is the last best place in America to live. See William Kittredge and Annick Smith, *The Last Best Place: A Montana Anthology* (Helena: The Montana Historical Society Press, 1988).

tories worthy of scholarly attention. During his career he published *Apron Full of Gold: The Letters of Mary Jane Megquier from San Francisco, 1849–1856* (1949), *Cattle on a Thousand Hills* (1941), *The Irvine Ranch of Orange County, 1810–1950* (1952), *Isaias W. Hellman and the Farmers and Merchants Bank,* with Frank B. Putnam (1965), *March of Industry,* with Osgood Hardy (1929), *El Molina Viejo* (1950), and *The Place Called Sespe: The History of a California Ranch* (1940). A masterful writer, Cleland used personification with great skill, letting the "good, stout walls" of the old mill of Mission San Gabriel declare the true romance of California's past.[5]

Cleland and Hardy's *March of Industry* was the first survey of the state's economic history, and Cleland's monographs made their mark. But after World War II the market for college-level California histories boomed: the modern educational textbook wars had begun. John Caughey, another Bolton student, entered the fray in 1940 with *California.* In Caughey's vision, California was part of the American West, yet international in scope. He went beyond the political and the economic history of the state to emphasize social and intellectual elements. Cleland countered with *California: From Wilderness to Empire* in 1941. A condensed version of the Chapman-Cleland two-volume work of the 1920s, this was a textbook targeted at the college market. Soon even the great professional historians had competition.

In 1949 Carey McWilliams published *California: The Great Exception.* Though McWilliams, too, was an attorney, he did not write from the evidence-gatherer perspective of Hittell. Rather, McWilliams was a New Dealer from the 1938 administration of California governor Culbert Olson. To McWilliams, California was an exceptional place granted seemingly limitless resources, but also a place in need of socialist solutions to its manifold social problems. His book was thought provoking but, not surprisingly, partisan.

As the first wave of "baby boomers" hit college in the 1960s, the soaring textbook market welcomed two of the enduring survey histories of the state. Andrew Rolle's *California: A History* (1963) was comprehensive and balanced. A student of Cleland and Caughey, Rolle brought the best of both to his work and added substantively to the subject. In 1967 Berkeley's Walton E. Bean penned *California: An Interpretative History,* which offered professors and students a discursive but highly interpretative version of Californians' accomplishments and enduring problems. Subsequent editions of both books remain part of today's textbook menu and are used in colleges and universities throughout the state.

But Rolle and Bean were not alone in the 1960s. In 1968 Ralph J. Roske gave us *Every Man's Eden: A History of California,* a work more romantic than analytic. William H. "Hutch" Hutchinson's *California: Two Centuries of Man, Land and Growth* (1969) was highly interpretative and colorfully written. Yet another journalist turned historian, Hutchinson placed heavy emphasis upon natural-resource exploitation and technology. Hutch did not advocate a single interpretation; rather, he explored numerous complex topics without championing an overarching theme or conclusion. California was too complex to fit the confines of singular interpretative constructs, even his. Howard A. DeWitt pushed the interpretative envelope even further with *California Civilization: An Interpretation* (1979). Adopting the currently fashionable conflict model of history, DeWitt concentrated his words to emphasize the plight of the farmworkers, plead the case of political dissidents,

5. See Gordon Morris Bakken, "Robert Glass Cleland," in John Wunder, ed., *Historians of the American Frontier: A Bio-Biographical Sourcebook* (New York: Greenwood Press, 1988), pp. 191–8.

and castigate racists. There was plenty of conflict here, but was anything else happening? Readers and reviewers were at a loss to say so.

Amid the post-Vietnam War critique and new left-history movement of the 1970s, some authors maintained the steady course of survey history. Warren A. Beck and David Williams produced *California: A History of the Golden State* (1972), a balanced survey drawing upon the strengths of its two prolific authors. Beck also published with Ynez D. Haase a *Historical Atlas of California* in 1974. Dividing their work into 101 sections, the historian and the geographer mapped and explored California's cultures and geography. Even the Mariposa Indian war of 1850-51 found its map and narrative presented for students of history. While Rolle and Bean maintained their market shares with new editions, the historical world was slowly atomizing amid intradisciplinary conflict and a multidisciplinary challenge. Now the largely unsung participants in California history demanded recognition, and new histories of women, African Americans, Mexican Americans, and American Indians were desperately needed.

In 1988 Richard B. Rice, William A. Bullough, and Richard J. Orsi, colleagues at California State University-Hayward, offered *The Elusive Eden: A New History of California.* The authors structured their text to provide both narrative and analysis, incorporating bibliographies to display the amazing explosion of historical literature on California. They presented California history in ten parts, featuring three chapters within each part. The first chapter of each part was a narrative about a person, critical event, or historical theme. Here the authors were confronting the traditional historical problem of how to organize history: chronologically or topically. More narrowly, the problem was how to present a narrative that would keep the students' attention in one chapter while helping them to grasp broader themes in two substantive chapters. To stimulate thought, the book was peppered with feature essays surveying a topic and asking a question such as "Were the Big Four 'robber barons' or public benefactors?"[6] Like the works of Rolle and Bean, the *Elusive Eden* went into subsequent editions and is still popular today.

Later in this volume, we will ask you to look at the meaning of California history. Perhaps the most important contemporary work asking this general question is Kevin Starr's multivolume history. Starr uses biography extensively to try to arrive at the meaning of California in a philosophical sense, much as Royce had done. Any student of California's social or cultural history must consult the body of work by Starr.[7]

Andrew Rolle's fifth edition of *California: A History,* published in 1998—thirty-five years after the original—blends cultural history into a rich tapestry heavily interested in the development of communities, both urban and ethnic. Shorter and more focused than earlier editions, Rolle's fifth edition explores the essential aspects of California history, coupling narrative with extensive bibliography, maps, and illustrations. Questioning the accepted facts of the past, Rolle broadens our reach in searching for California's meaning in our terms as well as the nation's.

6. Richard B. Rice, William A. Bullough, and Richard J. Orsi, *The Elusive Eden: A New History of California* (New York: Alfred A. Knopf, 1988), p. 248.
7. Kevin Starr, *Americans and the California Dream, 1850-1915* (New York: Oxford University Press, 1973); *Inventing the Dream: California Through the Progressive Era* (New York: Oxford University Press, 1985); *Material Dreams: Southern California Through the 1920s* (New York: Oxford University Press, 1990); *Endangered Dreams: The Great Depression in California* (New York: Oxford University Press, 1996); *The Dream Endures: California Enters the 1940s* (New York: Oxford University Press, 1997).

So, too, must we begin to ponder our approach to learning California history, asking questions that require critical thinking and careful, yet creative, research. In the process, we will learn both a good deal about what is in California history textbooks and about the vast world of historical information and interpretation outside the texts.

Through the use of this book, you will learn to master research and writing skills, hone your ability to think critically, and better understand California and your place in it. Best of all—regardless of your major field of study—when you have acted as a historian to complete the tasks that this book holds out, you will be better qualified to participate in this state's vibrant political and economic life. This is history's true gift. We hope you will accept it.

Teaching California History

We historians are fond of saying that all of us are products of the past and that the past is prologue, but beyond these slogans we strive to help students acquire a sense of the past that allows them to place their own experience within California's and the nation's, to overcome provincial notions of meaning.

But how do we go about this? We teach. We profess. That is, we take the wealth of knowledge contained in printed sources and bring it to students in lectures, discussions, and collaborative learning projects. To help us, we choose for our students textbooks, learning guides, and monographs that we think will further their understanding of the subject matter, sharpen their critical-thinking skills, and enhance their ability to express themselves verbally and in writing.

To promote critical thinking, we teach students how to analyze documents and place them in historical context. We want students to recognize that history provides evidence for and a form of argument about causation in the past. We also promote skills in reading, though history is not unique in this skills focus. Textbooks, whether descriptive or analytic, ground students in the basics of California history. The factual foundation displayed in a textbook represents years of work by hundreds of historians who have "interrogated" historical evidence and interpreted its meaning. The "proof" of that work is found in the footnotes that grace the pages of the textbook or the list of titles in its bibliography.

We also cultivate our students' research skills. In this information age everyone is bombarded by words, numbers, and images, yet as historians it is clear to us that much of these data do not equip us to answer questions about the past. Rather, we must study all events, old and new, in a context that evolves from immersion in the literature of history. Here we historians clearly have lead time over our students. We have completed undergraduate and graduate studies. We have read widely in the process and continue to read most of the new literature in our field. Now we want to start you down the same path, well aware that your journey this semester (or quarter) will of necessity be a short one. We want you to understand how to conduct historical research, in the process acquiring skills you will take to the workplace, to the reading of a newspaper editorial, to a Friday evening discussion, or to politics on the street. We see no limit on the application of these skills, for countless students have returned from "real life" to tell us how important they have been to them in their careers.

In addition to helping students learn to conduct research, we historians strive to help students express themselves in writing. Analysis of data means little without interpretative expression, so, naturally, we stress the importance of good writing skills. A poorly written message may be no message at all. Custer's Last Stand at the Little Big Horn River in 1876 is a case in point. In July, the U.S. Seventh Cavalry Regiment divided forces—with Major Marcus A. Reno overseeing three companies, Captain Frederick W. Benteen in command of three other companies, and

General George Armstrong Custer with five companies—in an attack on an American Indian village of eight thousand people. Sioux and Cheyenne warriors counterattacked. Seeing Reno's skirmish line under fire, Custer wanted Benteen's troops, packs, and ammunition brought forward into battle as quickly as possible. He motioned to his orderly trumpeter, Giovanni Martin, to carry the message. Lieutenant William W. Cooke, a Canadian, scrawled Custer's order on a scrap of paper and sent Martin to Benteen. The message read: "Benteen. Come on. Big Village. Be Quick. Bring Packs." The message bearer could hardly interpret the message because English was his second language.[1] Benteen did not advance to join Custer. Most of us know where Custer is buried. Was bad writing his downfall? Obviously there are numerous other questions that have been asked about the Battle of the Little Big Horn, but we cannot escape the issue of clear written expression. This book asks you to write a good deal and focuses on the nature of good writing. One of the reasons many history majors are good writers is the simple fact that most historians believe that writing is important. (By the way, many employers maintain the same position.)

Historians also advance the discussion of history. One approach we take is the Socratic method: simply stated, the instructor spends class time asking questions, which students answer out loud. Some instructors lecture to the class, asking questions based upon the lecture as well as the assigned reading. Others go beyond the scope of the classroom and the textbook to ask students questions that call upon their general knowledge, in this way expanding the context of the discussion. California history does not, and never did, exist in a vacuum. Rather, events taking place in the United States and the world influence events unfolding in California.

For example, a consideration of the rise of the wheat industry in antebellum California might involve asking a simple question: How did the wheat producers get their product to market? Students using present-day knowledge might answer the railroad, but others, aware that the national railroad had yet to reach California, would know to look further. Students knowing something about present-day wheat ships might suggest that the grain was handled in bulk. But those with knowledge of agricultural implement technology would posit that the wheat was by that time handled in bags. After putting all the facts together and considering the history of transportation systems, students eventually could surmise that wagons took bags to docks along watercourses to be transshipped to San Francisco Bay for loading upon ocean-going vessels. One answer, or fact, leads to another question, eventually setting the context for the rise of the bonanza wheat industry of Northern California.[2]

Some professors promote collaborative learning. Here students work in groups to research and write term papers. Another objective of collaborative learning groups is the mastery of readings in the class. For those of us educated in the 1960s, we call the structure a study group. We all knew that the group depended upon the mastery of each member, and that if any one member failed to produce, the group's knowledge and understanding was proportionally diminished.

Disappointed with one class's performance on an examination, Professor Bakken held up the textbook and reminded his students that they were required

1. Robert M. Utley, *Cavalier in Buckskin* (Norman: University of Oklahoma Press, 1988), p. 186.
2. Some students considering the question might start research with James P. Delgado, *To California by Sea: A Maritime History of the California Gold Rush* (Columbia: University of South Carolina Press, 1990).

to know certain details of history. Although he had previously told them the nature and extent of their responsibility to know certain persons and their impact on certain events, the students had not heeded his warning, their inattention to detail resulting in point deductions on their exams. Professor Bakken then picked up the 1965 U.S. Army field manual on booby traps (FM 5-31) and asked what the consequences might be if certain details of this text were ignored by its readers. One student immediately grasped the point, "You are dead!", he responded. Another student smiled knowingly. He was a veteran of the First Cavalry Division in Vietnam, 1969–72. For him, the lessons learned in another decade translated well in 1996. From then on, Professor Bakken referred to attention to detail as the lesson of I Corps. Still, without context, even the lesson of I Corps has little meaning.

Experiments in textual analysis and effective written expression have received differing evaluations. At the end of the nineteenth century, the lyceum meeting was an adult lecture-discussion course intended to advance reformist ideas. In theory, a lyceum paper assignment forced army officers to write, present, and respond to criticism. Matthew F. Steele, a low-ranking officer, offered this evaluation of a U.S. Army lyceum meeting he attended in February 1896: "I never heard such a constipation of ideas in a flux of words."[3] However, Zenas R. Bliss, another low-ranking officer trying to move up in a stagnant peacetime army, thought the lyceum papers useful because "writing causes carefulness of thought."[4] Your authors tend to agree with Bliss. One of the objectives of the exercises in this book is to help you learn how to analyze text from primary as well as secondary sources. Another is to stress to you the importance of the clarity of expression. Granted, we may have differing views about the utility of the exercises, but as you progress through the book, your skills inventory will grow.

3. Matthew Steele to wife quoted in Edward M. Coffman, *The Old Army* (New York: Oxford University Press, 1986), p. 277.
4. *Ibid*, p. 276.

Exercise

Read this story entitled "Grand Jury Inquest" from the Jan. 4, 1855 edition of the *Los Angeles Star.*

Three Men attacked by Robbers.

PLACERVILLE, December 23d.
The *Mountain Democrat,* extra, says: We received the following startling intelligence last night after our paper had been worked off. Rocky Canon, the place of the tragedy, is a deep and almost inaccessible canon about forty miles North of this place, near Todd's Valley, and uninhabited.

ROCKY CANON, December 20, 1854.—No officer having been within a convenient distance to attend to a case of emergency that has just happened near our isolated camp here, the undersigned constituted themselves a coroner's jury, and held an inquest over the deceased bodies of twelve men that were killed within a mile of our camp, on the 19th inst., a full account of which we deem it our duty to publish. Three of the undersigned were eye witnesses of the whole scene, though too far off to give aid in any way, and the rest can readily vouch for their veracity. On yesterday, 19th inst., three men who afterwards proved to be a Mr. Jas. C. McDonald, of Alabama now deceased; a Dr. Bolivar; A. Sparks, of Mississippi, and Capt. Jonathan R. Davis, of South Carolina, were travelling on foot on a trail within a mile of our camp, to prospect a vein of gold bearing quartz some 20 to 30 miles north of this place. As they were passing the base of a mountain, three of the undersigned being out on a hunting expedition on its side, saw a party of men concealed in the bushes near the trail, spring up and commence firing at them. Mr. McDonald had fallen dead. He had a pistol shot before he was even aware of his danger. He and his party had nothing but their revolvers. Thomas Sparks shot twice at the banditti, and then fell severely wounded.

In the meanwhile, Capt. Davis, who was the first to commence shooting in defence of himself and party, in an instant after the first volley of the robbers, being still unhurt, he kept up an incessant firing upon them with his revolvers, every ball forcing its victim to bite the dust until all the loads of both parties seemed to have been discharged. The four surviving robbers made a charge upon Capt. Davis, three with bowie knives and one with a short sword or sabre. Capt. Davis stood firmly on his ground until they rushed up abreast of him within about four steps. He then made a spring upon them with a very large bowie knife; warded off their blows as fast as they were aimed at him; gave three of them wounds that soon proved fatal. Having wounded the other one very slightly, and disarmed him by throwing his knife in the air in warding off a blow, as this last man expressed in a tone of gratitude before his death, Capt. D. went to work at once tearing up his own shirt and binding up the wounds of the living, of both his friends and enemies. On an examination of the persons of the deceased of those that commenced the attack on Capt. D. and party, we discovered papers, carefully concealed in their pockets, purporting to be a copy of laws and bye-laws by which they were governed.

The last of this band has just died. His wound he thought himself but slight and in a fair way of recovery until within the last hour, and corroborated all the evidence proven by the papers in his pockets. Signed by W. C. Thompson and 16 others.

Another letter dated Rocky Canon, Dec. 20, to Wm Henderson, Placerville, states:—"Yesterday we had quite an exciting scene happen within a mile of our tent—while two of my partners and myself were taking a hunt over the hills—we heard the report of guns below us, and saw two small parties shooting at each other. Convinced that they were strangers, we hesitated for a moment before we ventured down to them—a feeling of duty however, soon prompted us to hasten down. On approaching we saw two of a little party of three whom we had noticed following the trail unobserved, some half hour previous, fall in the fight and the remaining one, a man somewhat above the medium height, whom we could readily distinguish from all the rest by his white hat, fighting bravely for his life; approaching still nearer, we were surprised at the eight of eleven men lying stretched upon the ground, seven of them dead, belonging, as they afterwards proved, to a party of robbers, and one only of the party of three so suddenly fired upon from the bushes by robbers. Three of the wounded robbers having died last night, we had ten of them to bury. One of them survives, who will probably recover; he is marked, however, for life, having lost his nose in toto, and the fore finger of his right hand. Seven of them were shot through the head. The surviving one who seems to be but little hurt, says that their band was composed of two Americans, three Frenchmen, five Sydney men, and four Mexicans, and they had just commenced operations, having killed six Chinamen three days ago and four Americans the day before yesterday. Although we counted 28 bullet holes through Capt. Davis' hat and clothes—17 through his hat, and 11 through his coat and shirt—he received but two very slight flesh wounds.

Yours truly,
JOHN WEBSTER
To Wm. HENDERSON, Esq., Co. Surveyor, Placerville.

Placerville, also known as "Hang Town," ca. 1849. Courtesy of the California History Room, California State Library, Sacramento, California.

Name   Instructor   Date

Analyze the Text

1. What Happened to Captain Jonathan R. Davis and his party? Break down the report into its component parts: Who? What? Where? When? How?

_____

_____

_____

_____

2. Identify the witnesses:
A. Party 1:

_____

B. Party 2:

_____

3. Identify the "banditti."

_____

4. Prior to this incident, what had the banditti done?
A. In writing:

_____

B. To prior victims:

_____

5. What did the witnesses do?

_____

Put the facts in historical context:
6. What was California like after the Gold Rush?

_____

_____

_____

_____

_____

 Note: Obviously your textbook will help you form your answer.

Name _____   **Instructor** _____   **Date** _____

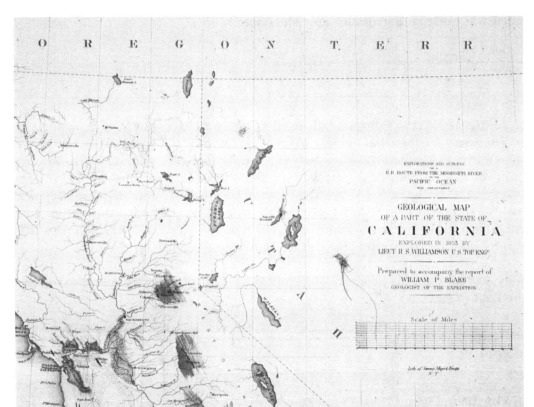

Geological map of a part of the state of California explored in 1855 by Lieut. R. S. Williamson, U.S. Top. Engineer. Roy V. Boswell Collection for the History of Cartography, University Archives and Special Collections Section, California State University, Fullerton.

TO GO DEEPER:
To create a specific context for the event you might go to the library to consult Roger D. McGrath, *Gunfighters, Highwaymen, and Vigilantes* (Berkeley: University of California Press, 1984). *John Boessenecker, Badge and Buckshot: Lawlessness in Old California* (Norman: University of Oklahoma Press, 1988). W. Eugene Hollon, *Frontier Violence: Another Look* (New York: Oxford University Press, 1974).

Optional Exercise

7. What was the West like in 1854? What was the content of the word "lawless"?

_____

_____

_____

TO GO DEEPER:
You may wish to consult John Phillip Reid, *Law for the Elephant* (San Marino: The Huntington Library Press, 1980) and *Policing the Elephant* (San Marino: The Huntington Library Press, 1997).

Optional Exercise

8. When Captain Davis and his assailants ran out of ammunition, what did he do?

_____

_____

Name _____ **Instructor** _____ **Date** _____

What was his legal duty under English common law?

_____

_____

Note: Richard Maxwell Brown tells us in *No Duty to Retreat: Violence and Values in American History and Society* (New York: Oxford University Press, 1991) that "should your opponent threaten you, you must not defend yourself with violence until you have attempted to get away—to flee from the scene altogether. If you are unable to leave the scene, you may not stand your ground and kill in self-defense. Instead you must retreat as far as possible from your enemy: to the wall at your back. Then, and only then—with the wall at your back and all retreat cut off—may you legally face your opponent and kill him in self-defense." p. 4.

Why do you think his peers did not hold Davis culpable for his failure to follow the English rule?

_____

_____

9. Why did the witnesses do what they did?

_____

_____

Note: John Phillip Reid's *Policing the Elephant* will give you some important hints.

10. Was the action of the witnesses believable?

_____

_____

11. What models did they have for their actions?

_____

_____

12. Why did the newspaper print the documents? Are there any other legal notices in the newspapers of the day?

_____

_____

_____

Name _____   **Instructor** _____   **Date** _____

13. Was the fact that the gang wrote rules for their enterprise unusual?

_____

TO GO DEEPER:
See Bruce H. Mann, "Tales from the Crypt: Prison, Legal Authority, and the Debtors' Constitution in the Early Republic," *The William and Mary Quarterly* 51 (April, 1994), pp. 183–202. John Phillip Reid, *Law for the Elephant* (San Marino: Huntington Library Press, 1980).

Optional Exercise

14. Are there any factual discrepancies within the text?
Enumerate them.

_____

_____

_____

15. What are some other questions you might ask of the text?

_____

_____

_____

_____

Name _____ **Instructor** _____ **Date** _____

Thinking Critically

We know that the authors of textbooks have taken a variety of approaches to the writing of California history and continue to revise their work to reflect the rapidly expanding historical literature and marketplace of ideas. California history is far more inclusive today than it was in the 1940s. During the 1960s, when Professor Bakken was studying at the University of Wisconsin, many scholars challenged the accepted nature of history and its interpretation. Some asked whether the study of great men, that is the narrative of history in terms of presidents and other powerful (usually white) figures, was a meaningful exercise at all. Others asked why blacks and women were largely ignored in the consideration of American history. Where were the Asian Americans and Mexican Americans in the tapestry of history as represented to students? These questions stimulated a generation to explore new materials and create new histories of America. In the process, California history blossomed, its wealth of information on exactly these neglected people awaited the new historians. Fortunately, California had—and still has—a wealth of research facilities deeply rooted in its rich historical soil. The Huntington Library in San Marino, perhaps the finest historical research facility in the United States, contained millions of historical documents, including photographs, rare books, beautiful specimens of nineteenth-century architecture, and priceless works of art. The Bancroft Library on the campus of The University of California–Berkeley housed Bancroft's research materials as well as splendid manuscript collections. The shelves of the state archive and the California room of the state library in Sacramento groaned with seldom-searched pages. All this combined with the holdings of county historical society libraries and university library special collections spread a veritable feast on the researcher's table. Working with the myriad available documents, the new historians applied a changing methodology and explored new mechanisms of inquiry.

To understand historical thinking is, in part, to walk with Clio, the muse of history, as well as with her modern fellow travellers, political scientists, economists, sociologists, and geographers. First, all researchers must locate the documents they think will pertain to their subject, but that does not make a history. Once one of Professor Bakken's students found a box of letters in an attic; he hoped to use them in order to write a master's thesis. The found documents were business letters involving events that had transpired over a twenty-year period, but there were only seventeen of them. Though the letters cited names, places, dates, and the terms of business, the student could find nothing more about the author or his business despite four months of research in newspapers and business directories. Without context, explaining the letters and their possible meaning was a lost enterprise. Perhaps other such letters will turn up some day and find their way into an archive, creating a larger context for interpretation. In this book, your authors have located documents for you to analyze but challenge you to go beyond the texts to forge your own interpretations.

After locating the documents pertaining to an event in question, historical researchers read them to try to determine what happened. The exercise in Chapter Two started you down this analytic path. As you probably noted in completing that exercise, not everything was evident upon a first reading of the document, particularly in light of the questions asked in the exercise. As Marc Bloch observed "the deeper the research, the more the light of the evidence must converge from sources of many different kinds."[1] Marc Bloch, 1886-1944, was the founder of the Annales School of historiography. He forged linkages between traditional history and the social sciences, particularly anthropology and cultural geography. Bloch maintained that history could be understood beyond political and diplomatic affairs to include the lives of common people. He insisted that the questions asked of historical documents determined the nature of historical inquiry and that documents were not objective sources, for the people who created them had a particular purpose in mind. As Bloch would attest, locating a single document gives a historian an opportunity to find meaning, but the task goes far beyond that single piece of paper.

As researchers, we must ask questions, or interrogate the documents in order to reconstruct the past in a way that gives it meaning.[2] Here historians make a number of assumptions that must be carefully delineated and qualified before we go on to the Chapter Three exercises.

As historians we assume that few events of historical significance are caused by any single factor; rather, we assume that historical events are the product of multiple factors. Custer is not buried at the Little Big Horn simply because he could not write clear orders. It was a factor. Benteen's inability to interpret Custer's order and the inability of the message bearer to articulate Custer's intent also were factors. But the list hardly stops there. The leadership of Sitting Bull and Crazy Horse were factors, as was a lack of good reconnaissance on Custer's part. Firepower was a factor: the American Indian forces were better armed. Based on his past experience, Custer made faulty assumptions about the resolve of the enemy to stand and fight amid a cavalry charge: the American Indian forces not only stood their ground, they launched a massive attack. The list goes on, as does the literature regarding Custer, Sitting Bull, Crazy Horse, and seemingly every element of the story. Custer's Last Stand is fixed in the American mind, but historians continue to disagree about a variety of issues regarding the event.

As historians we assume people matter. We look at personal choices in historical context. The immersion of the historian in that context fosters sophisticated analysis and interpretation. In the distant past, we assumed that great men mattered most. Nationally, we venerated the great presidents. In California, we started writing our history by retelling the glorious accomplishments of pioneers. These were mostly white men who made a name for themselves by winning public office or becoming wealthy, or both. We also glorified the violence of pioneers who created a new "civilization" in their own image, largely ignoring that their success came at the expense of Californians of Hispanic and American Indian descent

1. Marc Bloch, *The Historian's Craft,* translated from the French by Peter Putnam (Manchester, U.K.: Manchester University Press, 1954), p. 67.
2. There is adequate literature on techniques of doing this task, but Robert F. Berkhofer, Jr. *A Behavioral Approach to Historical Analysis* (New York: Free Press, 1969) still offers an excellent place to start. As an alternative, see Robert F. Berkhofer, Jr., *Beyond the Great Story: History as Text and Discourse* (Cambridge: Harvard University Press, 1995). Berkhofer's change of position was, in part, stimulated by doubt about objectivity in historical analysis. See Peter Novick, *That Noble Dream: The "Objectivity Question" and the American Historical Profession* (New York: Cambridge University Press, 1988). Novick's observations fit very well into the post-modern attack upon the canon of history as practiced by generations of historians.

who, of course, were hardly uncivilized. Vigilantes too made wonderful pulp for the print media. As mentioned, in the 1960s scholars turned the lens of history away from the pioneers, the politicians, and the popular tribunals. They still acknowledged the great men, but they also started to declare that the common man and woman, whether black, white, brown, yellow, or red, had a hand in making California history.

We assume that ideas have an impact on people, that ideas in context influenced events. Look back at the Chapter Two exercise and again ask why men did more than bury the dead. In other words, why did they consider it their "duty" to conduct an inquest and record and publish their findings? California's history is riddled with ideas about popular sovereignty, race relations, the authority of the people, gender roles, the efficacy of business regulation, and access to power. California also has its share of different religious beliefs bouncing across its historical court, whether utopian communities of the nineteenth century or custom-computer cadres seeking to leave their "vehicles" for another world. All of these must be accounted for in historical context to give content to the words and meaning to the ideas.

We assume that economics is a factor in human actions. You probably have heard of people "voting their pocket book." And when your credit card bill gets a sudden boost or your variable-loan bill spikes, you understand why Wall Street is so obsessed with changes in interest rates. In the late nineteenth and early twentieth century, some Californians questioned the economic power of railroads and worked hard to regulate them. Some accused corporations of gouging consumers. Some even believed that banks were an engine of the devil. We might ask whether that idea flowed from political ideology, theology, or economic theory. We do know that California is a world-class economic power and that agriculture plays a great role in that status. Some Californians believed that the growers became wealthy on the backs of minority field workers, first Japanese and then Mexicans. Others think the growers became wealthy on the backs of California taxpayers by using state-subsidized water to raise silos full of crops, which were, in turn, purchased by taxpayers. Notice that both versions of grower wealth are predicated on the assumption that all growers became wealthy.

As historians we assume that technology changes peoples' lives.[3] But we must be careful here. Consider the following: mechanization on the farm increased productivity; computers are time-saving devices; faster cars get people to work more quickly; the World Wide Web speeds research in California newspapers of the 1850s. If you look carefully at these four statements of faith, you will find that not all can be verified statistically or even in your own experience. But we do know that electricity *changed* the way people lived in California and that medical technology *changed* the quality of life for many Californians. Again, we must be careful when trying to match what we assume about technology with historical events.

We assume that we can quantify historical facts and use statistics, computer models, and construct behavioral models to support historical inquiry.[4] History has become multidisciplinary and welcomes the methodologies of economics,

3. See Raymond H. Merritt, *Engineering in American Society, 1850-1875* (Lexington: University of Kentucky Press, 1969). At page 60 Professor Merritt also noted the importance of communications skills for the engineers who would change America: "Just as the curriculums at Rensselaer and Stevens required four years of training in composition as well as an understanding of the contemporary languages of Western Europe, so also the technical press urged engineers to speak and write with clarity. Effective communication was central to explaining plans, promoting new projects, and issuing instructions to subordinates and subcontractors."
4. For some examples of the potential for quantification see Robert P. Swierenga, ed., *Quantification in American History: Theory and Research* (New York: Atheneum, 1970). Lee Benson, *Toward the Scientific Study of History* (Philadelphia: J. B. Lippincott Co., 1972). The enthusiasm

John Dustin Bicknell, Los Angeles pioneer attorney. This item is reproduced by permission of The Huntington Library, San Marino, California.

political science, and sociology into the tool kit a historian uses to construct an analytic narrative. When we have economic statistics at our disposal, we can run them through a computer to determine whether nineteenth-century California farmers were being over-charged by the railroads. With the voting record of the legislature before us, we can enter the yeas, nays, abstentions, and absences into a computer to create a matrix of meaning. We can compile neighborhood statistics, county records, and state population numbers to tease out the changing nature of the family. We can even use numbers to question the validity of a newspaper editorial asserting that Santa Barbara's Mexican-American population was responsible for a disproportionately high rate of crime. By consulting the arrest records and court records of the county, one historian found that, in fact, whites in nineteenth-century Santa Barbara were more frequently arrested and convicted for crime than Hispanics. The use of statistics has great potential, but numbers alone seldom explain *causation*.

We assume that certain institutions, whether the family or the court system, matter to people and influence their behavior. Within institutions, we assume that certain groups operate to exert influence. Whether an extended family disciplining a child or a political party working to pass legislation, groups of two or more people commonly gather to enforce institutional values.

We assume that geography and the environment shape history. Remember the historians who pictured California as Eden?[5] Just where in the state and when exactly did this "Eden" exist? When looking at the Central Valley and Imperial County, we see no "Eden" until the water is delivered. The coffee houses of San Francisco might have been edenic for poets of any century, but did Death Valley ever take on the edenic vale? Nonetheless, California is a state of great contrast, and its environment is a real and imagined factor in its history. Water was and is the life blood of human enterprise in California. You cannot pan gold without it. You cannot make steel without it, and you certainly cannot grow tomatoes without it. But while water is life, its use and distribution are matters of law and, even more certainly, the stuff of politics.

Finally, as historians we assume that inertia is real and that people will continue to do what is familiar until something pushes them off the dime. Seeking to explain change is very interesting; yet when we ask why someone did not seize the moment to make a difference in history, we must respect the power of inertia. Put more simply, we know that people are conditioned to do what they find most comfortable. Remember, continuity in history is the ground zero from which we establish and measure change.

---

for quantification waned by the late 1980s largely because the claims of some of its ardent practitioners fell short of expectations. Nonetheless, quantitative methods are accepted as standard tools of historical representation with analysis requiring more than numbers.

5. Kevin Starr's *Americans and the California Dream, 1850–1915* (New York: Oxford University Press, 1973) and *Inventing the Dream: California through the Progressive Era* (New York: Oxford University Press, 1985) are particularly useful in understanding the concept of Eden in California thought.

Exercises

Exercise 1

Read the following quotations from the delegates in the debates of the 1849 California Constitutional Convention.

The quotations below are reproduced from J. R. Browne, ed., *Report of the Debates in the Convention of California* (Washington, D.C.: John T. Towers, 1850): the corresponding page number follows each quotation segment.

William McKendree Gwin

"We are a new people, creating from chaos a government; left free as air to select what is good, from all republican forms of government. Our country is like a blank sheet of paper, upon which we are required to write a system of fundamental laws. Let the rights of the people be guarded in every line we write, or they will apply the sponge to our work." p. 116

"A mammoth State exchequer [would be] more dangerous to the liberties of the people than any foreign enemy that can approach our shores." p. 117

"Let us guard against infringing on the rights of the people, by legalizing the association of capital to war upon labor. This is the only country on the globe where labor has the complete control of capital. Let it remain so if we would be free, independent, and prosperous. If there are to be banks in the country, let us have private bankers, who, if they abuse the confidence of the people, can be punished by the law, indicted, and put in the penitentiary." p. 117

Winfield Sherwood

"If he desires to send a hundred dollars to Louisiana, he must either buy a bill of exchange or get a certificate of deposit, and if he gets that he will be very apt to select the association which will have the most credit to deposit his money with and draw his certificate from."

"It is a settled principle that the people will use the currency they like best." p. 119

Charles Tyler Botts

"My chief object, therefore, is to crush this bank monster."

"To put down banks, you must give the people a paper circulating medium."

"In a mercantile community, some circulating medium more portable than gold and silver is absolutely necessary to its existence."

"If you leave a loop-hole, this insinuating serpent, a circulating bank, will find its way through, because of the absolute necessity of the community for a paper currency." p. 125

Kimball Dimmick

"It is well known, that by the laws of the several States, where a person brings his slaves from a slave to a free State, they are free." p. 141

Oliver Wozencraft

"I will to vote against the admission of all colored men of the African race."

"We must never bring them in competition with our own labor. . . ." p. 145

Name   **Instructor**   **Date**

Edward Gilbert

"If you insert in your Constitution such a provision [barring all blacks from California] or anything like it, you will be guilty of great injustice. You will do a great wrong, sir—a wrong to the principles of liberal and enlightened freedom; a wrong to the education and feelings of the American people; a wrong to all the rights of government. You have said in the beginning of your bill of rights, that all men are by nature free and independent, and have certain inalienable rights. You go on to say that all men have the right of pursuing and obtaining safety and happiness; and yet sir, at the bottom of this you propose to say that no free Negro shall enter this territory—that he, a freeman, shall not enjoy the right which you award to all mankind." p. 149

Dimmick

"I conceive it to be of the highest importance that our judicial system should be made permanent in the first instance; that it should not be established with any view to a change at some future period; that when practitioners in these courts bring in their cases they may know where they are to end. This will prevent endless litigation, which would be the consequence if you have the courts vacillating; here to-day and there to-morrow; different judges on the same Court of Appeals, and the prospect of a change at any moment it may suit the wishes of the Legislature." p. 25

Morton Matthew McCarver

"I am in favor of having a fair trial before a jury; and whenever they have decided the case, if they say hang him, then hang him in thirty days, and do not give him an opportunity to escape. I do not desire that men shall be clear, after they have been found guilty before a jury of their peers, by any quibble of the law. I wish to see them justly tried, and if found guilty, then justly and properly punished." p. 226

Pablo Noriego de la Guerra

"There are many classes of men who have money, but who have not the capacity to carry on their affairs as they ought. These classes the lawyers pounce upon like vultures upon dead bodies; and although the lawyers know they cannot succeed in their suits, they urge them to go on."

"I think these classes require protection from the ingenuity of men who derive their income from the litigation which they are enabled to produce. What do they care how long the suits last, or what it will cost, provided they make money by it." p. 228

Francis Lippitt

"My own professional experience...[has been that] the influence of the poor man is much greater in the higher than in the lower courts." p. 229

Elam Brown

"The experience of fifty years has shown me that lawsuits are unprofitable to the litigants; they are usually attended with costs, loss of time, and many other evil results to both parties."

"I am opposed to the principle of holding out inducements for appeals in every petty case that may arise." p. 231

Lewis S. Dent

"No clause that you can introduce in the Constitution will prevent a man from fighting a duel, if it be in defence of his honor." p. 246

Gwin

"At this advanced period of the world, it is not necessary to say a word against this remnant of the dark ages."

"When you insert this provision in your Constitution, the fundamental law of the land, that a man is branded when he fights a duel, he quits it." p. 250

B. F. Moore

"There is one advantage to be derived from this provision, if you place it in the Constitution. It will at least afford men a pretext for not engaging in duels." p. 250

Lippitt

"Very good the gentleman tells you that he does not wish to have any provision made by law punishing a crime that does not involve any social degradation. That is precisely why we are called upon to introduce such a provision in our Constitution. It is the reason why ordinary laws passed by the Legislature have not accomplished the object." p. 252

Lippitt

"Laws shall be passed more effectually securing to the wife the benefit of all property owned by her at her marriage, or acquired by her afterwards, by gift, demise, or bequest, or otherwise than from her husband."

This matter is "more safely . . . entrusted to the action of the Legislature, than introduced at once into one Constitution, and form part of the fundamental irrepealable law of the land." p. 257

Henry Tefft

"It is the common cry to leave all these things to the Legislature, assuming that we are to have a Legislature that will look upon those matters as

Mexican women, Santa Barbara, circa 1880, photograph by C. E. Watkins. This item is reproduced by permission of The Huntington Library, San Marino, California

we do. I say that we have not only the right to embrace a provision of this kind in our Constitution, but that it is our duty. This is a matter in which not only the native Californians, but many of the new residents in this country, feel a deep interest. I do contend, sir, that every wife has a right, a positive right to the entire control of her private and personal property." p. 258

Henry Wager Halleck

"I would call upon all the bachelors in this Convention to vote for it. I do not think we can offer a greater inducement for women of fortune to come to California. It is the best provision to get us wives that we can introduce into the Constitution." p. 259

Botts

"I object to it on the general principle so often avowed in this Convention, that it is a legislative enactment; but I would object, also, to see it upon our statute books, because I think it radically wrong. In my opinion, there is no provision so beautiful in the common law, so admirable and beneficial as that which regulates this sacred contract between man and wife." p. 259

Lippitt

"The very principle [of married women's separate property] is contrary to nature." p. 261

"Creditors are certainly, if not deprived of the power of collecting their debts, put completely at the mercy of every dishonest man who has a wife, and can say that the property belongs to her." p.262

James McHall Jones

"The barbarous principles of the early ages have been done away with from time to time." p. 264

"Let the law secure to this class of women their rights, for they have no power themselves to secure them." p. 265

Botts

"If you introduce this clause, you must take care to carry along with it a speedy and easy way of procuring divorces, for they will come as sure as you live, as a necessary consequence. That very moment that you set up two heads in one family, you sow dissentions which lead to applications for divorces, and your courts and Senate chambers will be filled with them [divorce petitions]." p. 267

McCarver

"We possess an undeniable right to protect ourselves against this class of population [free blacks]."

"They will be a burden to us, and a drain from our treasury." p. 331

Andy at the sluice, a pioneer placer miner. This item is reproduced by permission of The Huntington Library, San Marino, California

Tefft

"Taxation in this country must be burdensome; and what I wish to urge particularly, is, that we should provide that that burden may rest as nearly equally upon the shoulders of all as possible." p. 367

Sherwood

"I am willing, therefore, to take this clause, because it is republican in its character and right in its nature—that property shall be taxed according to its value, and assessments made by persons acquainted with its value." p. 370

You will note that the delegates to the Constitutional Convention in 1849 did not stick to a single subject and that the issues were not always clearly delineated. Further, these quotations were chosen to give you an idea of how old some public policy issues of today are.

1. Read the information in your textbook describing the 1849 Constitutional Convention. Now analyze the passages above in light of this secondary-source information.

_____

_____

_____

Name   Instructor   Date

_____

_____

_____

_____

2. Identify five issues raised by the delegates in the 1849 convention.
Issues

_____

_____

_____

_____

_____

Compare the issues the delegates raised in 1849 to political issues of the 1990s in California (but stay away from the legislature here). Again, you may wish to consult your textbook.

_____

_____

_____

_____

_____

_____

_____

_____

_____

Optional Exercise

TO GO DEEPER:

Consult secondary texts other than your textbook on the period 1840–1857. Here you may wish to refer to the list of recommended books in the To Go Deeper sections in Chapter Two.

3. On separate sheets of paper, write an essay of three to five pages on the following question: To what degree did national events and issues influence the delegates to the 1849 California Constitutional Convention? Be certain to emphasize five issues raised by the delegates and consider them in the context of their time. Note: In focusing your attention on five issues, this exercise guides you to the formation of a good topic paragraph, which will alert the reader to the analysis to follow in the body of your essay. Before you begin your essay, you may wish to consult Chapter Eight: Writing California History. In it your authors explore some common writing errors.

Exercise 2

Read the following newspaper editorial and answer the questions that follow it.

LOS ANGELES STAR, MAY 13, 1873
ANOTHER FARMERS' CLUB.

A Number of farmers met at Gallatin Saturday, and completed the organization of a Farmers' Club…. The demand for a change of men and measures cannot be too strongly urged. This demand must come from the people themselves, wrought by their own honest convictions. It will not do to come from aspiring politicians; men who seek to obtain place, or a higher round in the official ladder, by declaiming against those who are occupying the coveted position. But when the people, the bone and sinew of the country, make the demand for reform, they will do so in such trumpet tones as will startle the corruptionists from their fancied security, armed though they be in triple brass. To have the people take the initiative in such patriotic measures, requires no secret conclave. It is the work for open day. It is the work for men. In such a matter there is no pretext for secrecy. It is a public duty, to be preformed in public, in broad daylight, every man participating to be known to all, to put his sayings and doings on record. All that is wanted is reform. We are crushed by corruptionists. We are borne down by taxation. We all know it—we all feel it. Why, then, seek the closed door, the sworn allegiance, the secret affiliation, to accomplish a public duty? Why these "Patrons of Industry?"—these "granges," and all the paraphernalia of secret societies, to effect a political reform? This is not the first time such a machinery has been set in motion to effect just such an object. We have had it in Native Americanism—in Know Nothingism. It failed in those instances—worse, it induced greater evils than it essayed to abolish. It will fail again. It will fail as "Patrons of Industry," as "granges," just as surely as it failed in previous secret political societies. Let the people meet, organize, agitate, combine, discuss—but let it all be done in broad daylight—with open doors—on a public platform, every man saying what he believes, what he wants—and recording his determination to effect his object by all and every constitutional means. Then we will know who are in the movement—what is wanted, and we shall be enabled to give our adhesion to the cause, based on intelligent reason and cogent argument.

1. What was the Know-Nothing Party? When did it exist nationally? Did California have such a party? What did the party stand for in public? In private?

_____

_____

_____

_____

2. Where did the "Grange" or Patrons of Husbandry originate? Who was its founder? What were its public goals at its founding? What were its goals in 1873?

_____

_____

3. During the nineteenth century, how many secret societies existed that had political aspirations? List the most prominent. What were their public policy goals? Why did they keep their membership secret?
Note: You may have to consult a good American history textbook to answer this question.

_____

_____

_____

4. Why is taxation an issue in 1873 in California? Be certain to distinguish between the rates of taxation and the burden of taxation. Who is (proportionate to income or wealth or both) paying the most in taxes?

_____

_____

_____

_____

5. What is a "corruptionist"?

_____

_____

Where did you find a definition for this word?

_____

Are there other possible definitions?

_____

If so, what are they?

_____

_____

6. What does the newspaper editor imply by calling the grange the "Patrons of Industry?"

_____

_____

7. By characterizing the "corruptionists" as armed in "triple brass," what Biblical allusion is the newspaper editor making?

_____

_____

What research resource did you use to determine this answer?

_____

_____

When a newspaper editor makes such a reference in a story, do you assume that the editor expects the reading public to readily identify the Biblical reference as well as the image it conjures up in the public mind?

_____

Why?

_____

_____

Instead of "triple brass," what language would you use to reach the reading public of today?

_____

_____

_____

Exercise 3

Read the following newspaper story and answer the questions that follow it.

Alameda Daily Argus,
February 19, 1906
SCHILLER TELLS ABOUT THE CASE

Otto Schiller, the defendant in the Schiller divorce case in San Francisco, in which Geo. MacRae, a former Alamedan appears to be more or less involved, now accuses McRae and Mrs. Schiller of a conspiracy to murder him. He alleges that the conspiracy was arranged to secure the $10,000 life insurance which Schiller carries and which is payable to Mrs. Schiller.

Schiller says:

"Mrs. Schiller, in her complaint, alleged that I complained when the baby cried. That is true. I am an electrical engineer in the employ of the Joshua Hendy Machinery Company. My work is trying on my nerves, and I need my sleep. I contended while the baby lived, and I still contend, that if my wife had given the little one the care to which it was entitled, it never would have been ailing.

But Mrs. Schiller spared little time for our baby. She was constantly occupied with her clubs. She wanted to become a society leader, to bear the reput[e] of being prominent in all women's clubs movements. Anyway, she spent the greater part of her time away form home with her club friends—and the baby looked after itself. Presently the baby died, and then she could spend all her time at the clubs without hindrance.

For the past three or four months, my wife has neglected her clubs for MacRae. We met him last summer at San Mateo, where he was introduced to us by Colonel Chaplin of the First Regiment, National Guard. Mrs. Schiller at once became infatuated with the former policeman, and frequently went out with him in the evening. I naturally protested. His attentions were too marked, and her affection too obvious.

One night I came home and found the two alone in Mrs. Schiller's bedroom. I protested as vigorously as I knew how, and MacRae struck me on the head with a revolver. Then I started to telephone the police, but my wife tore down the wire and rendered the telephone useless. She wept, expressing penitence and begged me not to expose her, saying it would disgrace her with her club friends, and I, hoping the infatuation would soon wear itself out, forgave her.

She often returned home late, after spending the evening with MacRae, and refused to speak to me, seeming to be lost in reverie. On such occasions she would sleep in the back parlor, leaving the bedroom to me alone."

The charges of Schiller about his wife being lured from home by the attractions of club life has caused a vigorous protest from club women across the bay, especially from members of the California Club to which organization Mrs. Schiller belongs.

1. Why did the newspaper print this story?

_____

_____

2. Do you believe Schiller's allegation that "the baby looked after itself?"

_____

_____

3. What was the function of women's clubs?

_____

_____

4. Why would club activity be attractive to women living at the turn of the twentieth century?

_____

_____

5. Would such activity have been perceived as a threat to men?

_____

If so, why?

_____

_____

6. To which economic class did the Schillers belong?

_____

How do you know?

_____

_____

7. What kind of marriage had Otto Schiller expected?

_____

_____

Mrs. Schiller?

_____

_____

Was the institution of marriage changing at the time?

_____

Name _____ **Instructor** _____ **Date** _____

How so?

_____

_____

Optional Exercise

TO GO DEEPER:

See Sara Hunter Graham, *Woman Suffrage and the New Democracy* (New Haven: Yale University Press, 1996).

Constructing Context

CHAPTER

Historical context has been mentioned a number of times in the preceding chapters, but it is important that you realize that context exists on many levels. To learn California history, to work within the canon of history, you should understand how historians construct explanation within contexts. You must recognize that when you interpret historical evidence, you do so in a personal context, albeit one increasingly informed by the reading of historical literature and, eventually, primary evidence. It is not easy to learn to use context, or contexts, to forge interpretation, but we will try to guide you through the process.

Often the first level in arriving at the context, or contexts, relevant to our subject of inquiry is a reading of secondary sources written by earlier historians. Say we wanted to conduct historical research in California politics in the late nineteenth century; to arrive at the first level of context, we might consult a California history textbook. In Chapter One, we saw that the authors of California history textbooks took two basic approaches to the subject. Either they focused on the people and events of California's past, or they put those people and events in a national context. The first approach was very useful for the first few generations of Californians trying to find meaning in their immediate past. Much of that history was self-referential and romantic, telling the tall tales of the pioneers battling against the odds to make the greatest state in the Union. The second approach put California's people and events in a larger historical context, one national, even international, in scope.

However, once we get past the survey textbooks and turn to specialized historical monographs in California history, we begin to appreciate California's particular nuances, which become more distinct precisely because we already have a sense of the larger (national) context in which California history exists. Looking at Hubert Howe Bancroft's history, we find a good deal on politics and politicians, yet the history is unsatisfying because much of it is episodic and contains little analysis. By moving on to Royce D. Delmatier, Clarence F. McIntosh, and Earl G. Waters, *The Rumble of California Politics, 1848-1970* (New York: John Wiley & Sons, 1970) and Michael P. Rogin and John L. Shover, *Political Change in California, 1890-1966* (Westport, Conn.: Greenwood Press, 1970) we find more incisive analyses. But even within the span of a decade, the study of nineteenth-century California politics has taken on new life, spawning a number of recent professional monographs. For example, in Philip J. Ethington's *The Public City: The Political Construction of Urban Life in San Francisco, 1850-1900* (New York: Cambridge University Press, 1994)[1], we find that the accepted paradigm of urban politics in the late nineteenth century—that it was boss centered, with political bosses

---

1. For the best synopsis of California political history see Spencer C. Olin, Jr., *California Politics, 1846-1920: The Emerging Corporate State* (San Francisco: Boyd & Fraser Publishing Co., 1981) and Jackson K. Putnam, *Modern California Politics,* 4th ed. (Sparks, Nevada: MTL, Inc., 1996).

running city political machines that controlled elections—unravels. Ethington demonstrates that San Francisco politics was far more complex, with newspapers and neighborhood interest groups playing a substantial role. Sometimes historians fail to include certain aspects of California history in textbooks and monographs, forcing your context to be broader than, say, Progressive politics in California.[2] Because we are now aware that California politics transcends labels, that urban machine politics did not dictate all political results, and that economic spoils was not the goal of all politicians, we are able to ask better questions of historical documents and current politicians. We would never have arrived at this level of inquiry, however, until we had read several different secondary sources, from the broadest context to the specific. In other words, historians immerse themselves in the secondary sources to find a professional context of explanation regarding a particular historical subject.[3]

The next level of context to consider is theater of operations. A political battle in California may only be a minor part of a national explosion of ideas and actions. As historians, armed with knowledge of secondary sources on the issues, parties, and players, we often have the distinct advantage of knowing more about an event than the participants. The politics of race in California, for example, focused first on Mexican residents, then black residents, Chinese laborers, Japanese farmworkers and merchants, Mexican farmworkers, and, finally, all of the above. The national debate centered on black Americans, yet race was the underlying issue, and California's brand of race politics shifted across time.

Head of Auburn Ravine in the 1850s. This item is reproduced by permission of The Huntington Library, San Marino, California.

2. For the complexity of Progressivism see William Deverell and Tom Sitton, eds., *California Progressivism Revisited* (Berkeley: University of California Press, 1994).

3. Marc Bloch also reminds us that the times in which the historian is writing history influences his product. "When the passions of the past blend with the prejudices of the present, human reality is reduced to a picture of black and white." *The Historian's Craft* (Manchester: Manchester University Press, 1954), p. 140. Inclusion and exclusion in text writing must be considered as well as the focus of the historian.

At this point, it is time to add our own research and interpretations to the collective pool of knowledge, to go beyond the published page and into the primary sources. At the simplest level, primary sources are documents created by the participants in or direct witnesses to a particular event. Typically, the author creates the document during or immediately after the event in question. The longer the author waited to create the document, the harder we must work to verify the author's memory. Letters, diaries, notes, paintings, photographs, or electronic records created at the time of an event render a more vivid portrayal than a reminiscence recorded fifty years after the fact. Also, we must read these documents critically and within the context in which they were created, acknowledging the cultural values or personal biases taken to the text by the author. Different witnesses to the same historical event may have "seen" very different things due to their cultural perspective.

While all of this is a lot to consider, we must also keep in mind that we historians (and historical researchers) bring our own experience to the reading of the text. In the 1940s historians told California's history as though women, blacks, American Indians, Asians, and Mexicans were virtually nonexistent. Being critically disposed to question the author's perspective allows us to put far more into the analysis of an event than did the author of a particular document. Being historically trained to be critical, we question the perspective of third-party observations, particularly newspapers due to their partisan linkages. Yet we can be assured that newspapers give us a glimpse of past events in the exact terms in which they were related to the readership, the people living contemporaneously with the events we are studying.

At yet another level, we know that words are important but that their meanings can change over time.[4] Therefore, we must judge words and the values they portray in the context of their time, *not ours*. This does not mean that we cannot make judgments; we must do so in the process of historical explanation. Looking at political rhetoric of the nineteenth century might give us pause because the language is overtly racist, but it will also give us a great deal of insight into the role of race in California politics.

The documents that follow contain language that powerfully resonates with national politics. Yet you will find that California added unique elements to the debate on race. Governor Weller's speech is reminiscent of the politics of Abraham Lincoln and Stephen A. Douglas. Weller alludes to popular sovereignty, a higher law theory of the Constitution, the natural extension of slavery theory, and an independent state constitutional ground for excluding slave labor. These issues are of the time when free labor made free men as a matter of political faith. You should remember these themes from your American history courses and be able to describe the linkages of rhetoric and context in 1857. So, too, Henry Haight's speech regarding the ratification of the Fourteenth Amendment to the U.S. Constitution. The Fourteenth Amendment passed both houses of Congress on June 13, 1866, as part of a comprehensive Reconstruction settlement package submitted by the Joint Committee on Reconstruction. Critical to the package was just equality of representation. Further, the Civil Rights Act of 1866 was already law, guaranteeing equality of property and other rights. You should note that Haight's primary concern was not the well-being of the freed slaves and their rights. To answer questions regarding citizenship, you may have to refer to a textbook or the *Los Angeles Times,* July 4, 1997, story on citizenship. More important, these exercises raise questions about race, equality, and rights in particular historic contexts.

---

4. See James Boyd White, *When Words Lose Their Meaning: Constitutions and Reconstitutions of Language, Character, and Community* (Chicago: The University of Chicago Press, 1984).

Exercise

Read the following primary documents and answer the questions that follow them.

1. *Los Angeles Star,* September 26, 1857 (The story reports the governor's speech.)
Public Meeting-Address by Gov. [John B.] Weller

"Let the people of each State regulate their own internal affairs, and not interfere with those of their neighbors, and by this means the good feeling harmony and prosperity of all would be maintained."

Regarding slavery . . . "I believe that a higher law than any legislation of man's forbids it—nature has forbidden it,—the climate, the productive capacity of the soil, will prohibit it. And after all, that is the true test for the extension of slavery. Wherever the climate renders profitable the employment of slave labor there will it find its way, and where nature has placed a bar to the production of those crops in the cultivation of which slave labor is found necessary, there it cannot be found necessary, there it cannot be introduced. Just so it was with us in California. We made our own fundamental law, excluding slavery—we were the best judges of what suited ourselves, and we were admitted into the Union with our constitution containing a clause forbidding the introduction of slave labor."

Characterize the political climate of America in 1857.

_____

_____

Optional Exercise

TO GO DEEPER:

See Kenneth M. Stampp, *America in 1857: A Nation on the Brink* (New York: Oxford University Press, 1990).

Weller's rhetoric sounds like that of which political party?

_____

Why? What are the words and phrases that convey political meaning to his audience?

_____

_____

_____

2. *Los Angeles News,* July 23, 1867
Speech of H[enry] H. Haight, Democratic Nominee for Governor, at the Grand Ratification Meeting, San Francisco, July 9th

"The whole essence of what is called the reconstruction policy of Congress, is indiscriminate suffrage, regardless of race, color and qualifications, coupled with a sweeping disfranchisement of the populations of ten States."

"Suffrage for all of every race and color is proposed to be engrafted upon the Constitution by the aid of those States, or enforced by Act of Congress as Mr. Sumner proposes."

"This is the cant expression, to indicate that all men shall vote, Asiatics, Africans and Indians. We believe that this doctrine if carried into effect would be our destruction."

"The Central Pacific Railroad with ten thousand Chinese laborers, could out vote the entire voting population of the mining counties, through which the road passes. Gangs of Chinese would be imported for their voting as well as working qualities."

To which Reconstruction policies is Haight referring?

_____

_____

_____

_____

Analyze his statement about racial minorities and suffrage. To vote, a person must be a citizen of a state or of the United States (Civil Rights Act of 1866). Could Asians become United States citizens in California in 1867? Were blacks citizens of the United States at this time? Were American Indians?

_____

_____

_____

_____

_____

_____

_____

If Chinese immigrants were not and could not become citizens of the United States in 1867, why is Haight concerned about "gangs of Chinese?"

_____

_____

_____

3. *Sacramento Bee,* July 18, 1871

A Dead Issue

Now this Chinese question is not an issue in this campaign. . . . The platforms of both parties are almost similar upon it. Both oppose the influx of Chinese into this country, but the Republican is the more positive, pointed and strong. The Democratic platform condemns Congress for not restricting the "importation of Chinese coolies," and declares against "Chinese immigration," while the Republican platform protests against "Chinese ever becoming citizens," and "demands of the Federal Government such treaty regulations and legislation as shall discourage their further immigration to our shores."

According to the news story, the Republican position benefits which economic interests?

_____

The Democratic position benefits which economic interests?

_____

Optional Exercise

TO GO DEEPER:

See Charles J. McClain, *In Search of Equality: The Chinese Struggle against Discrimination in Nineteenth-Century America* (Berkeley: University of California Press, 1994).

4. *San Francisco Chronicle,* July 1, 1875 (An excerpt of the California Democratic Party platform, which the *Chronicle* reprinted.)

THE DEMOCRACY . . . A Platform constructed of Reasonable Length."

". . . Fifth—We assert the traditional policy of the Democratic party in declaring it is the right and duty of the Legislature to regulate corporations, whether railway, gas, telegraph, water or otherwise; to limit their charges in the interest of the public, and to compel them to serve all citizens, without discrimination and at reasonable rates; and that when they refuse to do so we recognize the right and declare the intention of making them do so; and we further assert it to be the duty of the Government to preserve the waters of the State for Irrigation and other public uses instead of permitting them to be made the means of extortion and monopoly. . . ."

Why did the Democratic Party make such a declaration?

_____

_____

_____

What businesses did the Democrats see in need of regulation?

_____

_____

Was this proposal far in advance of political thinking at the time?

_____

_____

TO GO DEEPER:

See Gerald D. Nash, *State Government and Economic Development: A History of Administrative Policies in California, 1849–1933* (Berkeley: University of California Press, 1964). Katha G. Hartley, "*Spring Valley Water Works* v. *San Francisco*: Defining Economic Rights in San Francisco," *Western Legal History* 3 (Summer/Fall, 1990), 287-308.

Optional Exercise

5. *Sacramento Bee,* July 15, 1879
                    [Denis] Kearney on the Stump

It has been said that the presence of the Chinese among us caused the creation of this new party [Workingmen's Party of California]—and ostensibly that statement would appear to be correct . . . but the great impelling cause lies far beyond the Chinese. It is in our system of laws and in our customs. The speculation in office, the barbarism of modern commerce, the false system of currency that California insisted upon maintaining in order that the importers and other traders might be enabled to plunder the people, the high salaries paid to many officials, the increased and still increasing use of machinery in field and shop, the monopolization of the water and land. . . .

What did the Workingmen's Party do to change this situation?

_____

Were they successful?

_____

_____

6. The quotations that follow are reproduced from E. B. Willis and P. K. Stockton, *Debates and Proceedings of the Constitutional Convention of the State of California . . . 1878* (Sacramento, 1880). The corresponding page number follows each quotation segment.

Clitus Barbour

"The American idea . . . is a white man's government; a government of Caucasians, established by white men, and for white men." p. 649

Charles J. Beerstecher

"If we adopt this system of starvation, if we give them nothing to do, if we pay them no money, we finally reduce them to paupers, and when they are reduced to the condition of paupers, we have the right to transport them and send them out of this country." p. 657

James M. Shafter

"It has come down simply to this: if a large body in this Convention, and apparently a majority of it, correctly represent the people, these crude, unreasonable, and absurd claims must be allowed, and be by us carried, not into effect, but into this Constitution. An open revolution against all government is to be the effect. To give force to the argument we are distinctly told by one gentleman, and the idea is reiterated by others, that if this Convention does not yield obedience to these demands the streets will run with blood."

"When constitutional law has no longer any force in this State and country, when ignorance and violence shall undertake to rule us, it will become necessary to possess our souls in patience to endure the consequent disorder, or to provide those sharp remedies by which order and civilization vindicated at last the supremacy of rights." p.673

Given the first two statements, what is the objective of the Workingmen?

Barbour:

_____

_____

Beerstecher:

_____

_____

What standard for constitution-making does Shafter argue for in his rebuttal?

_____

_____

Optional Exercise

TO GO DEEPER:
See Carl Brent *Swisher, Motivation and Political Technique in the California Constitutional Convention, 1878-1879* (Claremont, 1930). Gordon M. Bakken, "Constitutional Convention Debates in the West: Racism, Religion, and Gender," *Western Legal History* 3 (Summer/Fall, 1990), 213-44.

Note: The following exercise on the California Greenback Party may test your knowledge of American third parties because answering the first part of Question Seven requires specific knowledge. If you are unsure of this aspect of American political history, consult a U.S. history textbook. More sophisticated analysis of the issues requires going deeper into the sources listed at the end of the question.

7. *Sacramento Bee,* September 23, 1882
Radical Greenbackers

Greenbackers are peculiarly well advanced in social and politico-economic science. In their platform ... they have packed much food for thought. They stand in the front rank of reform and human progress.... They desire that all taxes shall be raised by a graduated tax upon incomes, they desire the abolition of all laws for the collection of private debts, the purchase of the railway and telegraph lines by the people; that the hydraulic miners shall no longer be allowed to pour their tailings into the streams; that the soil shall be owned in limited quantities only, and then by none save those who live upon and cultivate it. . . .

The National Greenback Labor Party had its origins in what theory of money?

_____

Having a graduated income tax as the sole source of state revenue would benefit which interest groups?

_____

_____

The abolition of the collection of private debt would benefit which interest group?

_____

And create a detriment for which interests?

_____

At the time did other parties advocate the public ownership of rail and telegraph facilities?

_____

_____

Forcing the hydraulic miners to contain their mine waste and debris would benefit which interest groups?

_____

TO GO DEEPER:
See Robert L. Kelley, *Gold v. Grain: The Hydraulic Mining Controversy in California's Sacramento Valley, A Chapter in the Decline of Laissez-Faire* (Glendale, Cal.: Arthur Clarke, 1959). Donald J. Pisani, *From the Family Farm to Agribusiness: The Irrigation Crusade in California and the West, 1850–1931* (Berkeley: University of California Press, 1984). Gretchen Ritter, *Goldbugs and Greenbacks: The Antimonopoly Tradition and the Politics of Finance in America* (New York: Cambridge University Press, 1997).

Optional Exercise

8. *Sacramento Bee,* October 18, 1886
Bartlett's Little Talk
San Francisco Major Washington Bartlett, Democratic nominee for Governor
    "The great question of irrigation—the taking, storing and distributing of water—is seeking solution and its commanding the attention of thoughtful men in every section of the State. While it may be true that the necessity for a water

Copyright © 1999 Harlan Davidson, Inc.

system is confined to those sections of the State where the annual rainfall is least-to the great Sacramento, San Joaquin and Los Angeles Valleys-where the limit to the productiveness of the soil seems measured by the water supply, still the increased production of those sections, the increase of wealth and population certain to follow a development of the wonderful natural resources of these immense valley, would directly benefit every interest connected with the material advancement of the State."

How did Bartlett "know" that water projects in one part of the state would benefit all the people of the state?

_____

_____

_____

Optional Exercise

TO GO DEEPER:

See Donald J. Pisani, *To Reclaim a Divided West: Water, Law, and Public Policy, 1848-1902* (Albuquerque: University of New Mexico Press, 1992). Norris Nundley, Jr., *The Great Thirst: California and Water, 1770-1990s* (Berkeley: University of California Press, 1992).

9. *San Francisco Chronicle,* September 19, 1886

Speech of John F. Swift, Republican candidate for governor

"The Chinese, as individuals, came intending to spend only time enough with us to accumulate a certain amount of money, intending when this was obtained to hurry back to China with it, sending over to us another Chinaman as poor as the originally [sic] was to take his place, and thus to repeat indefinitely the depleting process; that the amount of capital thus removed from the country each year was making a draft upon our resources of a most serious character. We found also that the presence of the Chinese greatly retarded the incoming of white laborers with their wives and children, a class we so much needed."

Evaluate the factual basis for this argument. Did most Chinese return to China with capital?

_____

Were those Chinese who left California indeed replaced by new immigrants from China?

_____

_____

Did the existence of Chinese communities in the state retard white migration to California?

_____

_____

What sources did you need to consult to answer the last three questions?

_____

_____

TO GO DEEPER:
See Judy Yung, *Unbound Feet: A Social History of Chinese Women in San Francisco* (Berkeley: University of California Press, 1995). Alexander Saxton, *The Indispensable Enemy: Labor and the Anti-Chinese Movement in California* (Berkeley: University of California Press, 1971). Sucheng Chan, *Asian Americans: An Interpretative History* (Boston: Twayne Publ., 1991).

Optional Exercise

10. *Sacramento Bee,* October 24, 1894
Speech of J.V. Webster, Populist candidate for governor
"The banks no longer loan money on mortgages, but demand trust deeds; the average rate of interest on trust deeds and mortgages is not less than 10 per cent, while the increase in the value of the wealth of the Nation does not exceed 4 1/2 per cent. Nothing but ruin can come from such conditions. The cause for the prevalent distress does not lie in the tariff. It is because 30 per cent of the farms in the United States are mortgaged, and because of the high rate of interest and contraction of the currency. More money and cheaper rates of interest are wanted."

Is Webster's solution consistent with Populist demands in other states?

_____

_____

What is the difference between a mortgage and a trust deed? How is the bank advantaged by holding a trust deed rather than a mortgage?

_____

_____

TO GO DEEPER:
See Gordon Morris Bakken, *The Development of Law in Frontier California: Civil Law and Society, 1850–1890* (Westport, Conn.: Greenwood Press, 1985).

11. *San Francisco Chronicle,* October 31, 1898
Single Tax is an Issue
"[James G.] Maguire and his Democratic backers have sought to make the California people believe that the single tax is not an issue of this campaign, but the "National Single—Taxer," the official organ of the Henry Georgites, says it is. . . ."

Optional Exercise

What was the Henry George single tax plan?

_____

_____

Name   **Instructor**   **Date**

12. *Sacramento Bee,* September 20, 1902

The Oriental Invasion and Franklin K. Lane

"The Japanese are rapidly crowding the white man to the wall. In Florin the Japanese have made themselves master of the berry industry and now control fully nine-tenths of the acreage devoted to it.

What will be the future condition of the workingman in this State, when California is thoroughly Japanned—a condition that is rapidly coming?

Franklin K. Lane, Democratic candidate for governor, said "If the Japanese continue to come in in large numbers they also should be rigidly excluded. . . ."

Who loses economically if the Japanese take over the berry industry?

_____

Who gains?

_____

Who, exactly, does the "workingman" to which the author of the document refers represent?

_____

Optional Exercise

TO GO DEEPER:

See Cletus E. Daniel, *Bitter Harvest: A History of California Farmworkers, 1870–1941* (Ithaca: Cornell University Press, 1981).

13. *Sacramento Bee,* September 11, 1906

The Democratic Platform

The party goes on record with a declaration that franchises be granted only for limited terms according to absolute needs.

The platform demands that the State take all legal and proper means to encourage transcontinental railroads entering California. One-road monopoly is denounced.

The platform urges the withdrawal of unappropriated waters of streams, and that they be held for public use and not for private corporations. The practice of private corporations going to the headwaters of streams and appropriating the waters, as is now done in many instances, is condemned.

The public ownership of street railroads is favored. Disapproval is expressed of municipalities giving away their streets for railroad purposes without deriving adequate returns therefor.

The platform builders recommend that the State board of Equalization, the State Board of Railroad Commissioners and all similar bodies be abolished as being practically useless, for the reason that they do not perform any real public service. In the place of these, one Commission is urged to deal with all public institutions.

Why did the party take such a stand on franchises? Note: For a hint, see Gerald Nash's work on this question. Why is the party concerned about street railroads? Compare the situation in San Francisco and Los Angeles.

_____

_____

_____

_____

_____

_____

_____

_____

_____

_____

TO GO DEEPER:

See Winston W. Crouch and Beatrice Dinerman, *Southern California Metropolis: A Study in Development of Government for a Metropolitan Area* (Berkeley: University of California Press, 1964). James R. Vance, Jr., *Geography and Urban Evolution in the San Francisco Bay Area* (Berkeley: University of California Institute of Governmental Studies, 1964). Andrew Rolle, *Los Angeles: From Pueblo to City of the Future* (San Francisco: MTL, Inc., 1995), pp. 165–80.

Optional Exercise

14. *San Francisco Chronicle,* September 23, 1906
    Speech of James Norris Gillett, Republican candidate for governor
    "We shall do all within our power to get started in our broad and fertile valley's irrigation projects, under the supervision of the general Government so that the broad acres therein contained may support a large and prosperous population, thus adding greatly to the wealth of the State. We believe in . . . the conservation of our waters and the encouragement of mining . . . the improvements of our harbors and waterways for the purpose of cheapening transportation. . . ."

James Norris Gillett. Courtesy of the California History Room, California State Library, Sacramento, California

Name   **Instructor**   **Date**

Who does Gillett expect will pay for water projects and transportation improvements?

_____

15. *San Francisco Chronicle,* November 3, 1910

Speech of Hiram Johnson, Progressive Republican candidate for governor

"We still stand by the issue we took in the primary campaign nearly eight months ago when I started out in a little machine in the northern part of the State and went preaching the gospel of ousting William F. Herrin and the Southern Pacific from the politics of California. We want a government free from these bosses, one that is for the people and one that is free from the domination of railroads."

How long had this political complaint about the railroad been part of party rhetoric in California?

_____

_____

Optional Exercise

TO GO DEEPER:

See William Deverell, *Railroad Crossing: Californians and the Railroad, 1850-1910* (Berkeley: University of California Press, 1994).

Evaluating Evidence

In Chapter Four we explored fifteen primary-source documents and suggested a variety of secondary sources useful for your exploration of the context of historical documents. Most of the primary-source documents you considered were extracted from newspapers. You also pondered statements made by delegates to the 1878–79 Constitutional Convention. In this chapter we will explore the evaluation of historical evidence at a higher level of sophistication. You probably noted that many of the questions in the last exercise asked for an evaluation of the factual basis for a statement or for an evaluation of the benefits and detriments of public policy formation. Now we will go deeper into the nature of historical evidence to sharpen further your critical-thinking skills.

Again, we must keep in mind the nature of primary sources. These are documents created contemporaneously with the historical event they portray. Some examples of primary sources are newspapers, letters, diaries, business records, and government documents such as constitutional-convention debate transcripts, court and police records, legislative bills, statutes, and administrative rules. Photographs, films, maps, paintings, drawings, and even buildings are considered primary sources.

At far left is the second Inyo County Courthouse, completed in 1873. The building recalled eastern designs and was inviting to the public, the front door only four steps from the ground. It was the first building insured by the county; it burned to the ground in 1886. To the right of that picture is the third Inyo County Courthouse, which was completed in 1887, with an adjacent stone vault for storage of the paper products of the law. Like its predecessor, this building was easily accessible; once again, the law was not far above, or out of reach, of the common person. Both photos, courtesy Eastern California Museum Collection.

Regardless of its form, every primary source is subject to interpretation and its authenticity must be verified.

We need to know that a given document was indeed created by its stated author at a particular time or place. Newspapers usually bear the name of the editor and the date of publication on their front page, and many articles bear a byline, identifying the person (often a reporter) who wrote the story. Letters, too, usually reveal the name of the author (the sender) as well as that of the intended reader (the addressee); also, letters often bear the addresses of both parties as well as the date on which they were written. If any of these elements are missing from the document, it is up to us, the historical researchers, to try to reconstruct the relevant data. A diary entry made twenty years after the occurrence of an event does not carry the same weight as a letter or diary entry made on the day of the event. Further, we want to know that a supposed witness truly was in a position to observe the event in question. If so, this too adds weight to the document as evidence. Although it is easy to authenticate newspapers, many personal letters, and most government documents, we need to move beyond the name, date, place, and subject matter to assess the meaning of the document. Marc Bloch observed that "for a piece of evidence to be recognized as authentic, method demands that it show a certain correspondence to the allied evidences."[1]

In the case of newspapers, even after we have noted the authenticity of the source, we must read the document and assess whether the coverage of the subject matter is accurate. Because many newspapers were blatantly partisan instruments and not objective tellers of fact, even with an article or editorial in hand, we must look for corroborating evidence of the event. Looking at another newspaper of the day might help, but that may simply provide us the view of the other party. Remember, since the time of Thomas Jefferson, political parties have used the press to get their ideologies before the people in the form of "news." In the first half of the nineteenth century, Andrew Jackson took this use of the captive press to new heights. Then, later in the century, party newspapers were joined by corporate-owned newspapers. Not surprisingly, the controlling party candidate or the parent company always looked good in print, while the competition was likely to seem incarnate of some demon.

California's newspapers were often partisan, but some were clearly attempting an independent stance. In the nineteenth century, the *San Francisco Chronicle* was a Republican newspaper and the *San Francisco Examiner* was usually a Democratic instrument.[2] The *Alta California* maintained itself as an independent press and is an excellent comparative source for the period 1849–1891. The *Sacramento Bee,* under James and then Charles McClatchy, focused on the capital city and legislative matters, but it also provided another view of events in San Francisco and later Los Angeles. The paper even went to court to maintain its right to print the news; the *Bee*'s lawsuit established the right to print legal proceedings not barred by court order to public notice.[3] Our present view of the freedom of the press under law was formed by such litigation. When conducting research on many topics in California history you will find a wide variety of newspapers to review, but keep in mind the need to find other sources that verify "the news."

Accordingly, we want to find other sources that might help us interpret the meaning of documents. Here the old technique of immersion in the sources certainly helps. If you have read many pages of primary-source documents on a particular subject at a particular time by a particular author, you clearly have an edge

1. Marc Bloch, *The Historian's Craft* (Manchester: Manchester University Press, 1954), p. 120.
2. Phillip J. Ethington, *The Public City* (New York: Cambridge University Press, 1994), p. 22. Ethington puts the newspapers at the center of much of the politics of San Francisco. His discussion of sources and problems of interpretation in the introduction is excellent. Also see Frank L. Mott, *American Journalism: A History of Newspapers in the United States through 260 Years: 1690 to 1950,* rev. ed. (New York: Macmillan Co., 1950). Dan Schiller, *Objectivity and the News: The Public and the Rise of Commercial Journalism* (Pittsburgh: University of Penn. Press, 1981).
3. *McClatchy* v. *Superior Court,* 119 Cal. 413 (1897). On freedom of the press also see *In re Shortridge,* 99 Cal. 526 (1893).

in arriving at a contextualized and nuanced interpretation. That is what professional historians do. We use a context constructed from years of reading and research and our own discernment of what made sense at the time to find meaning in documents. We also learn the past meanings of words and recognize that meanings and forms of usage change over time.[4] Again, context and meaning are important when looking at any document, when considering the whole or even a single word.

Some liken the professional historian to a private detective or an attorney, for both of the latter gather evidence for their clients. The private detective develops evidence to facilitate the client's ability to make a decision. The police detective develops evidence to determine whether a crime has been committed, whether a particular person or persons committed the crime, and whether the evidence is sufficient to bring a criminal complaint against the suspect or suspects.

Historians and those acting as historians (this means you) must perform a similar task when conducting original research. First, we gather those primary sources that we suspect of containing evidence—in light of our reading in the secondary sources and formulation of context. Once we have read through and taken notes on those piles of paper, photographs, maps, and books, we go to our "evidence room" or "laboratory," most likely a desk or simple work space, and sift through the evidence in the hope of establishing a set of particular historic facts. Some facts are easy to develop. What was the date of an event? Who was there? What happened? Then we come to the hard part: what caused the event? Now we need to explain the event in context, perhaps linking it to a theme in history, in order to form our own interpretation. Think about the statement that California is an equal opportunity racist state. So far, how many of the documents that you have read in this book would support that statement? We can see racism on the face of some of them. But can we conclude that those documents prove the validity of the statement? Or do we need to go deeper to look for the existence of other documents that indicate that at the same time other Californians were working equally hard to fight racism and promote racial equality and harmony? In seeking meaning, we need to seek balance. But how do we arrive at that balance?

The fourth Inyo County Courthouse, completed in 1921, took on classical architectural designs. Now the law would be imposed and announced from an edifice of Olympian dimensions; the people, it would seem, were now well beneath the law. Courtesy Eastern California Museum Collection.

4. James Boyd White, *When Words Lose Their Meaning: Constitutions and Reconstitutions of Language, Character, and Community* (Chicago: The University of Chicago Press, 1984).

Going back to the court of law analogy and the historian as attorney, we know that the standards of evidence in criminal trials and civil trials differ.[5] In the criminal case, the prosecution must prove guilt beyond reasonable doubt. In the civil trial, the plaintiff must prove the case by a preponderance of the evidence. In other words, if there is one small feather's greater weight on the plaintiff's side, the plaintiff must prevail. That's what the law requires, but in many cases, criminal and civil, there is a jury. And the jury may be convinced by some particular aspect of the evidence rather than the whole of the evidence. Here we may find that the behavior of jurors does not follow the letter of the law, but jurors understand that they must rule based on the evidence presented. Similarly, even with standards of evidence, we historians know that our jury—all of our colleagues in the field as well as the rest of the readership of our work—is extremely critical and that the quantum of evidence presented as well as our argument for a particular explanation of causation or meaning must be compelling. We also know that we make different cases based on different kinds of evidence at different times. Was Bancroft concerned with the history of women or minorities in California? Hardly! Would we consider writing a history of California today without including women and minorities? Hardly! Yet how much, what quantum of evidence, should we bring to our argument about the evolution of women's rights or racism in California? While the jury is still out on that question, there is a body of scholarly work analyzing the pervasive racism in our society and on women's rights.

Again, we return to the balance issue and look for as many primary sources as possible to give our issue historical life. We need to marshal evidence from those who advocated a certain position as well as from those who opposed it. We need to bring in the evidence of multiple sources, to use the broadest brush to paint a clear and vivid historic mural.

But even with all these sources in hand, we still must assess the weight of each as evidence. Historians and the law of evidence favor direct observation of events. We want to find key witnesses to events whose recollection corroborates that of others, as well as the evidence in other documents on the event.

For example, on January 31, 1968, Vietcong troops launched the Tet offensive, attacking five of six major cities in South Vietnam, thirty-six of forty-four provincial capitals, and other targets, including the American embassy in Saigon. The U.S. and South Vietnamese forces had been caught off guard, but they managed to launch defensive strikes. When the offensive ended, more than half of the attacking Vietcong troops were dead and the allied forces again controlled the cities. When the American people watched televised news coverage of the Vietnam War, they saw firsthand the grisly images and heard television commentators on the scene say that the Tet offensive heralded the defeat of South Vietnam and its U.S. supporters. Then a statement was issued by another person on the scene, U.S. general William Westmoreland, who claimed that the Tet offensive actually was a great victory of American arms. But Westmoreland's words fell on deaf ears; the American people, including President Johnson, believed what they had seen and heard on TV—albeit in tiny pieces. Who was right? Obviously, the testimony of two eye witnesses to the same historical event can, for many reasons, be contradictory. And different cultural lenses can focus on different issues. Those who opposed the war in Vietnam clearly saw defeat flowing from Tet, while professional soldiers simply counted the bodies and declared a great victory. Perhaps all

---

5. Marc Bloch presents an alternative analogy of scholar and judge. In Bloch's terms, the judge is a civil law system judge acting without a jury and with specific limitations imposed by the state. *The Historians's Craft* (Manchester: Manchester University Press, 1954), pp. 138–42.

of these witnesses to history were telling the truth (in their context) when they created documents we now use to explain history.

Since even eye-witness observation can be colored by culture, experience, or role, how are we to assess historical documents created by those who did not have an eye-witness perspective? The lawyer would raise the hearsay rule when presented with such documents, citing them as inadmissible evidence. As historians, we know that what people believed to be true is often as important as what was true. Again, context is crucial to a historical study. For example, say the nation was in the throes of an economic downturn and you wanted to drum up support for a political agenda creating a massive federal welfare system. First you would have to convince the American people that the economic plight was so great that such drastic, federally funded social programs were necessary. One way to do so would be to send photographers out to the hardest hit areas of the nation to take the most pathetic portraits of Americans in need.[6] The New Dealers did just that when they sent Lorena Hickok out to create the images that convinced Americans of the depth of the Great Depression. Obviously, on this photographic tour she purposely did not visit the prosperous parts of the country.[7]

Hickok visited the poor farmers of Bottinueau County, North Dakota, as well as the migrant-labor camps of California. She took her photographs with a political agenda in mind, often posing her subjects to illicit an emotional response from viewers. Her photographs, nonetheless, are great historical documents of human suffering and evidence of government propaganda. During the time Hickok was photographing Americans suffering in the Great Depression, the residents of Conroe, Texas, were experiencing a period of economic growth and prosperity, and the residents of Northwood, North Dakota, were frequently on winter vacation in California, Washington, Texas, or Europe. The critical analytic point of these contrasting experiences is that images may not represent reality and that even long-held historical interpretations of historical events may be flawed.

Another aspect of evidence to which lawyers and historians pay attention is relevancy. To be relevant in court, evidence, in the light of logic, reason, experience, and common sense, must have, by reasonable inference, a tendency to prove or disprove a disputed fact, issue, or contention. The same rule of common sense applies to the evaluation of historical evidence. As a historical researcher, you have the burden of proving to the "jury"—others who will read your work—that the evidence you have presented is relevant. Say you are a historian who has researched the woman suffrage movement in California. After gathering a great deal of evidence and arriving at its meaning to form your own interpretation of the events, you present your paper to a classroom full of history students. After you read your paper, one student raises the issue of women and property rights . . . how is that related? Another questions the position of women on temperance in the nineteenth century . . . what does that have to do with voting? Yet another brings in all kinds of literature on abortion . . . how relevant is that issue to suffrage? What about race? The questions multiply, and you sense that relevance in history has a great deal to do with the questions asked and who is asking the questions.

6. Charles J. Shindo, *Dust Bowl Migrants in the American Imagination* (Lawrence: University Press of Kansas, 1997), pp. 38–54.
7. Gordon Morris Bakken, *Surviving the North Dakota Depression* (Pasadena: Wood & Jones, 1992).

The documents that follow involve the issue of woman suffrage. You may want to read all of the documents before answering the questions because the arguments in them offer extreme contrast. You should be particularly conscious of context because the issue of the vote for women was regional as well as national. The West led the nation, with states granting women suffrage in various forms long before the Nineteenth Amendment became part of the U.S. Constitution in 1920.

Exercise

Read the following documents and answer the questions that follow.

1. Cora Clement, *A Woman's Reasons Why Women Should Not Vote* (Boston: J. E. Farwell & Company, 1868), pp. 12–15.

Is it not conceded that woman's vote would not materially change the result of elections? Is it not conceded that the right of suffrage will be not help to her pecuniarily? Is it not conceded that the women who are looking to the right of suffrage for elevation, in any sense of the word, are looking in the wrong direction? Is it not conceded that the real wrongs of women, which lie within the reach of legislation, may be righted without her vote.

It is not to be denied that some of the laws in which women as a class, are interested, are apparently unjust.

It may be thought very magnanimous of the law to allow a woman, at her husband's decease, her wardrobe, and that of her minor children, together with the privilege of remaining in her husband's house forty days, and then, too, she can have the use of one third of the real estate. Why is she restricted to the use of one third? Think of this, husbands, whose wives by their industry and economy have helped to accumulate and save your property, Especially if your estate is small, what help will the use of one third of it be to her in her efforts to get a living.

Why the ruinous division of property when a man dies intestate. . . . It probably had not entered this woman's mind that there was a law which could deprive her of a part of her home. She had paid for it and thought it her own. It had been with a thankful heart that she was able to do so much to lighten her invalid husband's cares, that she had for years pursued her toilsome way. Now a distant relative of her deceased husband come forward, and claimed his share of the property. . . .

It suffices little that the law allows a woman to keep for her own use what she earns. Most wives expect to, and do, devote themselves to the work at home, so long as they are not driven by dissolute and niggardly husbands to the necessity of providing for themselves; so long as they are true to their best impulses, do they toil form choice for the common good; and husbands should not be in haste to arrogate to themselves the credit of having acquired all their property. Let them be just to the wives who have toiled as many hours in the day as themselves; and what have they had, or what have they to expect from their labor? It is not enough, that a man can, if he choose, make a will, providing amply for his wife in case of his decease. So long as "Men think all men mortal but themselves," so long they will die intestate; and their wives must suffer by their neglect. The plea that laws cannot be made to meet all cases, does not show clearly why laws cannot be made which would secure to widows the same rights in property which it allows the husband when the wife dies. Nor does it show why such a law would not be just and proper.

What type of source is this?

_____

Who was Cora Clement?

_____

_____

Briefly summarize Clement's argument.

_____

Is the title of this source misleading? Why?

_____

_____

What does it mean to "die intestate"?
Note: You may have to look this up in a legal reference source.

_____

_____

Is there a fallacy in Clement's argument?

_____

If so, what is it?

_____

_____

What is the right of survivorship?

_____

_____

When did women obtain property rights equal to those enjoyed by men? Was it before or after they obtained suffrage?

_____

_____

Name _____ **Instructor** _____ **Date** _____

Is Clement addressing a national issue, or one particular to California?

_____

_____

2. *San Francisco Chronicle,* July 28, 1870
Woman Suffrage Movement
"The first anniversary of the California Woman Suffrage Association was held last evening at Dashaway Hall. . . .
THE LITERARY EXERCISES
Were opened by the reading of a letter form Virginia City, written by Emily Pitts Stevens. Mrs. Stevens referred in glowing terms to the meeting of five undaunted souls which was held one year ago in a parlor in Jessie Street, and which then gave birth to the society which she had the honor of addressing. She pictured its wonderful growth and progress, but she said their path had not been all sunshine. They had been called to put to flight enemies within and without their ranks, but they had not swerved for the right. [Cheers.] They had been loyal to their watchword of "The Ballot and Justice." [Applause.]"

What type of source is this?

_____

Why are the women assembled?

_____

What did the women want from the political system?

_____

_____

Who do you think were the "enemies within and without" to which Mrs. Stevens referred?

_____

_____

3. San Francisco Chronicle, January 14, 1872
Female Suffrage and Woman's Rights
The Assemblymen were not inclined to give much notice of the wailings of the he-hens and female roosters; but, finally, they agreed to appoint a Committee to consider the questions. May the Lord have mercy on the Committee . . . if they don't make a favorable report they will surely get their eyes scratched out.

What type of source is this?

_____

What is the purpose of the statement?

_____

_____

What do the words "he-hen" and "female roosters" refer to in 1872?

_____

_____

4. *San Francisco Chronicle,* February 4, 1872
Woman Suffrage

It has been asserted (to look at the matter more seriously) by some of the advocates of woman's rights, that "no depraved or vapid women have ever yet identified themselves with this movement." This is not true; for the Eastern papers come to us every day filled with accounts of those asking for woman suffrage, who, at the same time, boldly avow themselves the advocates of free-love and other like abominations.

We feel convinced every pure-minded woman will shrink from any association with the movement, and from all who, in the sense to which we have alluded, desire to bring it about.

What type of source is this?

_____

Briefly summarize the author's argument:

_____

_____

What is the author's motivation?

_____

_____

_____

Assess the effectiveness of this anti-woman's suffrage argument.

_____

_____

Were similar arguments made to stop the Equal Rights Amendment?

_____

_____

Name _____ Instructor _____ Date _____

5. *San Francisco Chronicle,* February 15, 1872

THE TYRANT MAN.

His Shackled and Oppressed Slave, Woman.

Second Day's Proceedings of the Woman's Suffrage Association

Emily Pitts Stevens quoted: Let women stand up for their rights if they want them. She believed the men of this nation were going to help the women out in this thing. . . . It don't do to abuse the men. It don't pay to abuse they. We are only half civilized in this nineteenth century, anyhow. Men are doing a great deal better by the women than they get credit for. It is only necessary to impress upon them the absolute necessity . . . of giving to woman her rights and her proper position.

What type of source is this?

_____

Who is Emily Pitts Stevens?

_____

_____

Briefly summarize her argument.

_____

_____

_____

Assess the validity of her assertion that "men are doing a great deal better by the women than they get credit for."

_____

_____

6. *San Francisco Chronicle,* February 15, 1872

Women in Council

The woman-suffrage movement does not appear to gain strength as time rolls on. This is owning partly to its own nature, but more to the way in which it is conducted. It seems to gather round it all the eccentricities and absurdities of the day; all the odds and ends of the political world. We do not now allude to the vagaries of its Eastern apostles, or it is perhaps hardly fair to judge a movement by the excesses of its wildest supporters. . . .

The woman suffrage movement has assumed an importance during the last two years which we may safely predict it will never again possess. It tries to inaugurate a state of things which nature itself has not only pronounced against, but rendered impossible. Women, as a rule, can neither govern, make laws, nor fight, and it is better that they should not. Were they to be lost to their present sphere, the whole world would soon be reduced to a condition of savagery. Women are possessed of qualities of mind and body altogether distinct from those of men, and which demand and find a different field for their exercise. They cannot be men if they would, and cannot perform the work of men. Nor do we believe that, as a body, they desire to do so. Talk of women's rights! Do they not, with us, possess a right to the best of everything, and do they not exercise that right to the utmost? They are first in the home circle, the ball-room and the lecture-room. They have the best seats in the church, the theatre, and the street car. The last seem to be reserved exclusively for women. Men pay, but do not dare to claim a seat while a lady is present. So in everything. Women are really the rulers. Some, however, wish to be everything at once. Those ladies must not be in too great a hurry; voting and holding office have duties connected with them. They who vote must fight, must work. Will the ladies be anxious to play the latter part? We trow not.

What type of source is this?

_____

Briefly summarize the argument.

_____

_____

_____

What is meant by the statement "the woman suffrage movement had assumed an importance during the last two years...."?

_____

_____

This argument contains several misstatements of fact, even for the 1870s. Identify three.

_____

_____

_____

Despite these erroneous assertions, analyze why these statements could be persuasive.

_____

_____

_____

What do all six of the sources above have in common?

_____

Name _____ **Instructor** _____ **Date** _____

Why is this significant?

_____

_____

_____

7. *Sacramento Bee,* October 28, 1896

Woman Suffrage: Susan B. Anthony Greatly Encouraged by the Outlook.

Susan B. Anthony, who has just returned from an extended campaign trip through the southern part of the State, is much elated over the prospects of woman suffrage on November 3d. Wherever she went, she said the greatest possible interest was manifested in the question by those of all parties.

The workingmen especially showed great interest and Miss Anthony thinks that a large vote will be obtained from them in favor of the amendment.

The only organization up to date that has not approved of it is that of the liquormen. The natural justice in man is showing itself, and he knows that the best way to elevate woman and make her a true helpmate is to put the ballot into her hands.

What type of source is this?

_____

Who is Susan B. Anthony?

_____

_____

Why would the liquormen withhold their approval of the amendment?

_____

_____

What is meant by the term "natural justice"?

_____

_____

8. *Los Angeles Times,* October 14, 1896

A Woman Gives Her Views on Equal Suffrage

Of all the newspapers in Orange county, but one is owned and edited by a woman and that one is the *Orange Post,* published in the town of Orange. Mrs. Alice Armor is the lady who edits the Post and this is what she has to say under the caption of "Equal Suffrage. . . .

There is but one ground upon which woman can claim the ballot and that is the promotion of the general good. If there are strong reasons for believing or even fearing the concession of the right to vote may prove harmful, the concession ought not to be made. . . .

Name _____ **Instructor** _____ **Date** _____

Miss [Susan B.] Anthony's (center, seated) last visit to California, 1905. This item is reproduced by permission of The Huntington Library, San Marino, California.

Let the mother in the home surrounded by her children be acknowledged to be in her most fitting place, and let no laws be passed which shall force upon her duties in conflict with those which God Himself has entrusted to her and to her alone. Almost all occupations and professions and many public offices are open to such women, married or single, as wish to enter upon them and are fitted to do so. Let that suffice without forcing conditions which will be binding upon all women, no matter how unwilling they may be to undertake burdens which they feel to be unfitted to their shoulders.

What type of source is this?

_____

Who is Mrs. Alice Armor?

_____

Briefly summarize her argument.

_____

_____

TO GO DEEPER:
Consult the following secondary sources:
Jane Jerome Camhi, *Women Against Women: American Anti-Suffragism, 1880–1920* (Brooklyn: Carlson Publishing, Inc., 1994).

Optional Exercise

Name   Instructor   Date

Billie Barnes Jensen, "'In the Weird and Wooly West': Anti-Suffrage Women, Gender Issues, and Woman Suffrage in the West," *Journal of the West* 32 (July, 1993), 41-51.

Donald G. Cooper, "The California Suffrage Campaign of 1896: Its Origin, Strategies, Defeat," *Southern California Quarterly* 71 (Winter, 1989), 311-25.

Norma Basch, *In the Eyes of the Law: Women, Marriage, and Property in Nineteenth-Century New York* (Ithaca: Cornell University Press, 1982).

Marylynn Salmon, *Women and the Law of Property in Early America* (Chapel Hill: The University of North Carolina Press, 1986).

9. *San Francisco Chronicle,* March 2, 1907
Senators Vote on the Suffrage Amendment

California stands upon the very brink of woman suffrage. A few more judicious smiles, directed preferably to Senator Willis, their chief opponent, and the petticoated politicians may go home with laurels. . . .

Senator Willis, although opposed to fair voters, thought that this was lukewarm.

"I had expected to make myself unpopular with the ladies," said Willis, "by saying something against this measure; but there is only a half-hearted support. I want the women to stay where they are, and not come down to the level of mere men and mingle in politics. We can't trust the people. They will carry the amendment in a spirit of chivalry or else snow it under so deep that the ladies will be insulted. Politics, as we have seen it at this session is enough to ruin the reputation of a man. Imagine a lady sitting here and being called a looter. I am not speaking of the hard-eyed specimens of the sex, but God never intended women to be our equals, but rather our superiors."

Willis said that clubwomen were different from other women, and that it was only clubwomen who were in favor of suffrage.

What "place" does the senator advocate for women?

_____

_____

Where were women situated in the California society and economy in 1907?

_____

_____

_____

What, do you suppose, was Senator Willis's idea of a "hard-eyed" specimen of the sex?

_____

_____

_____

How were clubwomen different from other women in 1907?

_____

_____

10. *San Francisco Chronicle,* January 19, 1908

Women Unite for Suffrage: College Graduates and Those of
Professional Schools in Alliance

The Northern California branch of the Collegiate and Professional League for Equal Suffrage [CPLES] was organized yesterday with a charter membership of ninety members. The meeting took place in Century Club Hall, when a constitution was adopted. The intent and purpose of the society is for the education of women to the cause of suffrage and teaching them the logic and principles of it. The society is constituted only for women of college degree or professional women with diplomas for recognized institutions. . . .

Mrs. [Charles] Park spoke of the purposes of the league and its broadening influence in the life and condition of women saying that in Utah, Wyoming, and Colorado women were paid the same wages as men for the same grade of work. "The attainment of this cause means freedom, advancement and civilization just as much as the outcome of the battle against slavery did, and for this we must endeavor," she concluded.

———————————

The CPLES was an auxiliary of the National Woman's Suffrage Association. How many national organizations were working for woman suffrage by 1908?
Note: If you are unsure about the number of national organizations working for suffrage at the time, consult Glenda Riley's *Inventing the American Woman: An Inclusive History,* 2d ed. (Wheeling, Ill: Harlan Davidson, Inc., 1995).

_____

_____

What are the stated goals of CPLES?

_____

_____

Did you include goals beyond the vote?

_____

How are the CPLES clubwomen different from other clubwomen of the period?

_____

_____

_____

Name _____   **Instructor** _____   **Date** _____

11. *Santa Ana Daily Register,* October 21, 1909

Women's Organizations and the Public Press

The following paper on "Women's Organizations and the Public Press" was written by Mrs. W. L. Grubb and read by her on Tuesday last before the Woman's Club of Santa Ana:

But only within the last twenty years has the spirit of association seized upon the mind of womankind impelling her to establish societies and unions for the purpose of reform, along hitherto neglected lines, as well as to promote and stimulate social and intellectual intercourse.

This is an age of organization; we seem to realize more fully each year, that in union lies our strength, and that through it, we may accomplish all things. Woman in recent years has come in contact with our newspapers very largely through her charitable and reform associations, for today, as in the past, practically all the charities of the Christian communities are in the hands of women. Conventions are being held over the country for the purpose of promoting reform in penal institutions, establishing missions and rescue homes when needed; urging the adoption of better sanitary measures in our schools and public buildings; hastening progression along the line of civics and municipal improvement.

What did Mrs. Grubb mean when she declared the age of organization?

_____

_____

_____

How had other groups used organization to achieve specific goals in the political arena?

_____

_____

What penal reforms were under discussion at the time?

_____

_____

What were "rescue homes"?

_____

_____

What sanitation reforms were currently under discussion?

_____

_____

Did you look into public health as a concern of the Progressive movement?

_____

What is civics?

_____

_____

Why would people want civics education in 1909?

_____

_____

What was under discussion as "municipal improvement" at the time?

_____

_____

Did you look into Progressive positions on municipal administration?

_____

What about the American Socialist Party's position on municipal reform?

_____

12. *Los Angeles Times,* September 8, 1910

Many Women are Unable to Enter Stanford

Many women who came to Stanford this year with the expectation of entering the university have not been allowed to matriculate, and have either returned to their homes or entered the University of California. More than 200 co-eds to-be applied to the registrar for admittance, but of this number only 135 were admitted.

The rules of the university limit the number of women students to 500. This ruling is considered advisable principally because the intention is to keep the institution from becoming feminized.

Why were qualified women denied admission to Stanford?

_____

_____

What was the policy basis for this action?

_____

_____

Name _____ **Instructor** _____ **Date** _____

What does it mean when an institution becomes "feminized"?

_____

_____

Could the total number of women admitted or in attendance at any California university be limited today? If so, on what basis?

_____

_____

_____

13. *Los Angeles Times,* September 12, 1910

   SAYS WOMEN ARE SAVAGES: Desire to Vote Denotes Emotional Insanity"

Dr. Max Baff, a psychologist of Clark University, who believes that all women are fundamentally savage, says concerning woman suffrage:

"To put votes for women under the microscope, I would call the movement an outbreak of emotional insanity. What makes women talk on street corners? What makes them declaim from soap boxes? What makes them distribute handbills? Nothing but excitement," Dr. Baff declares.

"Do they really want the ballot? No; they just think they do. They ought to do men's work. They ought to dig the tunnels. They ought to run the street cars. They ought to begin right now to practice with the hammer and some nails.

And they are perfectly capable of doing these things. In foreign lands, women do hard manual labor. It is not considered degrading in localities where it is done. It would not be degrading here—if the women would do it; but they won't. They are looking for something easy.

What makes them want to vote? Hysteria. Their excited suggestibility. Women want to do what everybody else is doing. They follow the crowd. This whole movement is caused by a few women who excite other members of their sex. Because they come along and collect a crowd on the sidewalk and stand on a platform and say that they want the ballot, every woman who is listening thinks that she wants to vote.

If women want to vote, let us say, if they want to vote on an affair of the city street cleaning department they should first get a job and clean the street themselves. Physically, they would be able to do it. If they want to walk across a bridge whey ought to help build the bridge. Why can't they be carpenters and engineers and draughtsmen?

Why can't the men wash the dishes? Men do not want to wash dishes (this very emphatically.) There is no reason why they should do the work that belongs to women. You cannot make a woman out of a man, and you can't make a man out of a woman. That is the situation in a nutshell. The trouble is that women think that they can make men of themselves. As far as the actual performance of putting a ballot in a box goes, a woman is just as well able to vote as a man. A business woman should be allowed to vote as long as she prefers to remain unmarried."

What evidence does Professor Baff use to support his argument?

_____

Was there any evidence in 1910 that women did not want the jobs held by men?

_____

_____

_____

Were there any men in America doing dishes?

_____

_____

Why would the newspaper print this story?

_____

_____

What is the context of the times in terms of the suffrage campaign?

_____

_____

_____

_____

_____

_____

_____

_____

_____

TO GO DEEPER:
Read Manuela Thurner, "'Better Citizens Without the Ballot': American Anti-Suffrage Women and Their Rationale During the Progressive Era," *Journal of Women's History* 5 (Spring, 1993), pp. 33, 37–43.

Optional Exercise

Interpreting Evidence

Moving from evidence to interpretation is the most creative, yet challenging, task of the historian. Again, we are back to the question: what does it mean? Basically, the historian must exercise professional judgment and take a stand on the evidence he or she presents. The text the historian produces must contain clear and convincing evidence to support his or her interpretation. Commonly we find documentation of that evidence in footnotes or in the text itself in the form of evidentiary quotations.

Your authors believe that extensive multiarchival research in primary sources is a prerequisite to sound interpretation. Further, as Chapter Five stressed, students of history must be grounded in secondary sources to arrive at context. Only then can good questions emerge; only then is interpretation possible. With facts in hand, you can explore the meaning of an event. If you have completed the exercises in this book up to this point, you can easily understand how multiple meanings can exist simultaneously. This chapter introduces increasingly sophisticated views of interpretation and the use of statistics in interpretation. For some insight on the theory of historic interpretation, we turn once again to Marc Bloch.

Returning to the scholar/judge analogy, Bloch wrote that "they have a common root in their honest submission to the truth. The scholar records or better still, he invites the experience which may, perhaps, upset his most cherished theories." The good judge "questions witnesses with no other concern than to know the facts, whatever they may be. For both this is an obligation of conscience which is never questioned." But the two differ. "When the scholar has observed and explained, his task is finished." The judge, on the other hand, must "pass sentence."[1] Still, the historian has the more difficult duty in explanation because he or she needs to understand the context (the multifaceted mural) and explain causation in culturally nuanced terms. Both human behavior and the paper products of behavior—statutes, court cases, and rules—are historical evidence that must be considered amid the wealth of other documents.

Like Bloch, Robert F. Berkhofer Jr., a professor of history at The University of California–Santa Cruz, has made some important contributions to our thinking about historical analysis. In *A Behavioral Approach to Historical Analysis* (1969) he provided a model.[2] He acknowledged the need to analyze the internal component of human action, distinguishing what people said from what they did. He also set out some important assumptions about history. History, he maintained, was based on evidence interpreted by historians, leading him to the conclusion that

---

1. Marc Bloch, *The Historian's Craft* (Manchester: Manchester University Press, 1954), pp. 138-9.
2. Robert F. Berkhofer, Jr., *A Behavioral Approach to Historical Analysis* (New York: Free Press, 1969). The section that follows is drawn from this source unless otherwise indicated.

history is historiography. More simply, history is what historians say it is! Yet, the growing diversity of opinion on what history means as the century closes challenges this assumption. Berkhofer also contended that the past was an objective reality independent of the historian's consciousness of it. Hence, history could be reconstructed. Historians did, after all, have the advantage of hindsight.

A group of scholars called Postmodernists doubted that any universal or homogenous truths could be found, and they urged that scholars advance pluralistic views of reality. Historians like Hayden White and Michael Foucault took seriously Marc Bloch's suggestion that all historical documents were contextual and subjective. The Postmodernists argued that words are linguistically indeterminate and that we are better served by deconstructing historical studies in an attempt to reveal their subjectivity. Some Postmodernist scholars go so far as to deny the existence of any historical truth, but this extreme position is held by few serious scholars.

How best to overcome some of these limitations on historical interpretation? Berkhofer tells us that multiple variables must be considered in analysis. In moving toward interpretation, historical researchers need to consider human behavior. Our thinking must account for dynamic events, considering both the rational and the irrational. Complexity must be recognized. Historians must see people in situations and do their best to account for biological, psychological, social, and cultural factors. Berkhofer gives us useful rules for this type of analysis. The historian must determine the historical actor's interpretation of the situation, discover the actor's behavior in the situation, detect feedback to the actor, define the "real" situation of the actor as seen by observers, and trace the full consequences of the actions, be they anticipated by the actor or not. After comparing these elements of analysis, the historian then could attribute connections according to theories of behavior. One important caveat in the formula was the cultural lens.

This problem of cultural perspective is critical in California history because we have a multicultural past, present, and future. Berkhofer asked whether the historian could reconstruct a whole culture with reference to the reality people of the past perceived. He suggested that we divide the culture into its component parts, putting them back together in the process of writing history. In this approach, the first cut of analysis was to divide a culture into what people thought, what they did, and what they had. The second step was to decide what was knowledge at the time and what was belief. The same exercise must be accomplished by present-day historians. We need to understand the myths of the past and question the myths of the present, remembering all the while that in the past, people believed that they lived in a modern and enlightened era, just as we do today.

We must see historical actors and events in time. Berkhofer tells us that we must consciously date events and the observations of actors. But time itself may not be an exact thing. Some see it as linear and nonrepeating. Others think of it as a scale or a continuous succession of equally divisible moments moving ever from past to present. There is subjective time that is framed strictly in the actor-observer's terms, and there is cultural time that is more rhythm than unit, more event rooted than calendar based. Many "periods" of time or "eras" have been created by historians. For example, some historians date the antebellum period 1848–1861, while others deem it 1815–1861. Why are they different? Because periodization depends upon interpretations of causation. In this case both temporal designations were created by those searching to explain the origins of the American Civil War. For California, the antebellum period is relegated to 1849–1861, the time between the Gold Rush and the outbreak of the war. We also have the historical tradition of studying events as synchronic, a cross-section of the whole at one time, or as diachronic, a phenomenon through time. The most challenging part of writing history is trying to blend the synchronic and the diachronic into a narrative that provides meaningful explanation.

Berkhofer sets out the levels of historical explanation to sharpen our inquiry and enable interpretation. These levels flow from a series of questions: Who was it? What was it? When or where did it happen? How did it happen? Why was this who or what involved? Why did this happen when or where it did? Why did this happen in this sequence? With these questions answered in the process of historical research and analysis, we are able to move on to explanation and, ultimately, interpretation. In moving from evidence to historic fact and explanation, Berkhofer warns that quantification, the conversion of historical facts into numbers and their analytic manipulation, is no substitute for a carefully thought out set of questions.[3] Again, the right questions draw the historian closer to the issues of the day and an explanation.

A quarter century later, Berkhofer thoughtfully reconsidered most of his methodological and philosophical positions of 1969.[4] The contingent nature of the craft is now explicit. Documents were subjective and a historian's choice of documents to construct narrative was subjective. The great story based on grand narrative and singular causal factors was improbable. This pessimistic view of historical neutrality did not set aside the need for rigorous, multiarchival, and inclusive research. Nor did it did it dismiss the need to ask good analytical questions. Your authors believe that good questions rooted in professional inquiry of primary-source documents can produce informative explanation and meaningful interpretation.

The rise of the cliometricians in the 1960s gave the profession new hope of revealing patterns and meaning. Some of those hopes were realized through the application of statistical analysis, others were shattered. "Cliometrics" is a term used to define the use of computers, increasingly complex analytic programs, and inventive social science models to explain historical events. Going beyond statistical displays, many hoped quantification could simplify interpretation. The most important advances the cliometricians made are in the fields of legislative and economic history. In the former, scholars spent countless hours dissecting the speeches of United States senators and representatives to determine the meaning of actions in Washington. The traditional, linguistic analysis of politics usually led the profession to accept certain interpretations of political parties and political personages. Historians came to believe that people did what they said, that people's words mattered. Then the cliometricians took a look at what people actually did, running thousands of vote counts through a computer, to determine the true relationship between rhetoric and behavior. As Berkhofer noted in 1969, it was far more revealing to determine what people did than to focus exclusively on what they said they were going to do or claimed to have done. Allan G. Bogue was the most important cliometrician of the 1960s. He developed new methods of com-

3. Ibid, p. 314. Richard White, one of America's leading western historians, agrees, noting that "history is an act of interpretation, it is, among other things, a reading and re-reading of documents. Ideally, our methods are always comparative. We compare documents; we read them against each other. We order them chronologically. Deconstruction is, in a sense, what historians have done for a considerable time. We look for assumptions; hidden threads of connection; we probe for absences." Richard White, "Indian Peoples and the National World: Asking the Right Questions," in Donald E. Fixico, ed., *Rethinking American Indian History* (Albuquerque: University of New Mexico Press, 1997), p. 93.
4. Robert F. Berkhofer, Jr., *Beyond the Great Story: History as Text and Discourse* (Cambridge: Harvard University Press, 1995).

puter analysis and wrote two paradigm-shifting books in the 1980s.[5] His work showed that computer programs could measure the cohesion of a political party based on voting behavior and the content of legislation.

At the same time political historians were applying quantitative analysis, economic historians took to the mainframe and started to crunch a mass of numbers so large that it could not have been considered in the past, except, perhaps, as a lifetime study. The antebellum theory (a belief for some) that even had the Civil War not occurred, the institution of slavery would—if confined to the South and to agriculture—have died a natural death did not stand the test of computer analysis.[6] Further, studies of people over time can create a portrait of groups. Typically, historians isolate a profession, class, race, or gender for statistical study, find and gather the quantitative information, and use a computer model to create statistical tables to determine relationships as well as mathematical measures of significance. A case in point is a collective biography of nineteenth-century California lawyers, a cliometric study that shattered some conventions by revealing the subjects' true origins, education, place of practice, and specialization for each decade and county.[7] In short, numbers could portray both events and people where numbers could be found.

But even with computers to help us interrogate historical evidence, Berkhofer's caveat remains significant: quantification is no substitute for good questions. After the scholar has crunched the numbers, he or she still must interpret them and place the information they yield in a context, the analysis still must proceed from good questions asked of the evidence, and the answers to those questions must be integrated into the interpretative framework. Remember the question that asked who was responsible for most of the crime in Santa Barbara County, 1850–1900? According to the newspapers of that time, Hispanic residents were to blame for the majority of the crime in the county. However, if we put all of the arrest data, court records, and incarceration statistics into a computer program and compare names, dates, crime types, judicial outcomes, and the like, as Mark James Connolly did, we find that Hispanics did not, in fact, compose the majority of the criminally accused, convicted, or incarcerated.[8] Connolly's questions of Who? resulted in categories based on race; What? demanded categorizations based on the seriousness of the crime committed; and When? required specific dates and a longitudinal look at crime. Similarly, if we believed—as many did—that economic depression caused an increase in the crime rate in California, our minds would be changed by the statistical research of Lawrence Friedman and Robert Percival.[9] Their data dem-

5. Allan G. Bogue, *The Earnest Men: Republicans of the Civil War Senate* (Ithaca: Cornell University Press, 1981) and *The Congressman's Civil War* (New York: Cambridge University Press, 1989). Bogue's books demonstrated that very sophisticated computer analysis of easily quantified historical events such as roll-call votes as well as much more complex linguistic questions such as legislative intent could be quantified, analyzed, and interpreted through cliometrics.
6. Robert Fogel and Stanley L. Engerman, *Time on the Cross: The Economics of American Negro Slavery* (Boston: Little, Brown & Co., 1974). The authors crunch numbers regarding plantation income, slave population, slave prices, slave food production, and the like to produce six tables and forty-six figures representing analytic cliometric findings. The authors interpreted these findings to conclude that slavery would not have died out without westward expansion. Further, the record of black achievement under slavery was substantial.
7. Gordon Morris Bakken, *Practicing Law in Frontier California* (Lincoln: University of Nebraska Press, 1991), pp. 1–17.
8. Mark James Connolly, "Social Deviance in the Shadows of the Presidio: Crime and Punishment in Santa Barbara County, California, 1850–1900," M.A. Thesis, California State University, Fullerton, 1987.
9. Lawrence Friedman and Robert Percival, *The Roots of Justice: Crime and Punishment in Alameda County, California, 1870–1910* (Chapel Hill: University of North Carolina Press, 1981).

onstrated that crime rates in Alameda Country declined from 1870 to 1910, this despite two depressions. Crime and poverty had no positive statistical connection. Here again, the good question asked and set in context yielded a sound historical interpretation. The mantra of the twentieth century, that poverty breeds crime, failed to stand the test of statistical research, at least in Alameda County, California, for the period, 1870–1910.

While all of these examples of professional historical accomplishment make clear the possibilities of cliometrics, we must be able to interpret data in context to enable explanation. As is the case with linguistic evidence, when confronting numerical evidence you must ask whether the data you have gathered constitute a sufficient sample. This is critical: an insufficient sample can lead to erroneous conclusions. Looking at the crime statistics of Santa Barbara County, would a sample of data for the years 1850, 1860, 1870, 1880, 1890, and 1900—a 10 percent sample— be sufficient to consider the period as a whole? It sounds sufficient to statisticians, but a historian might ask whether the incidence of crime might have some relation to population changes, economic shifts, or ethnic demographics, which might require another study considering specific dates outside of the decade-by-decade method. But might the latter approach skew the numbers to reflect a research bias? What, then, would work? Naturally, a study of all of the years would be best. Whether or not such a sizeable and time-consuming study is a practical undertaking is another matter. Fortunately, for many historians it is.

Beyond sample size, you need to break the data down into its component parts, asking questions of each part before attempting synthesis and interpretation. Often the component parts are driven by the way statistics were kept. Furthermore, though statistics are a valuable source, they must be considered in a context necessarily involving other numbers, documents, and images to relinquish meaningful explanation. For example, the census records help with certain questions about gender, occupation, and family size. County histories frequently contain similar information on prominent local citizens, even though this information often is skewed to the rich, white, and male inhabitants of the place in question. Newspaper obituaries may provide more detail, but the evidence of any one source is not equal to that of the sum of all the sources. As always, the richest analysis proceeds from multiple sources.

Another consideration is the time period for analysis. For example, finding that American Indians were arrested significantly more often in San Diego than were persons of any other single ethnic group in 1852 may simply indicate that a large number of American

Patrick Reddy, flamboyant criminal defense attorney, delegate to the 1878–1879 California Constitutional Convention, Inyo County mining law expert, and San Francisco attorney. Courtesy Eastern California Museum Collection.

Indians overindulged in spirits one Saturday night and ended up spending a week in the city jail. Looking at the category of criminally accused (American Indian) over the decade of the 1850s or even over the span of entire nineteenth century may reveal that in San Diego, American Indians were arrested less frequently than were the members of any other single ethnic group. But even if your study were relegated to the year 1852 alone, you would need to see the data in the context of its time.

In sum, statistics are important, but to arrive at interpretation the numbers must be appraised in the broadest possible context and in relationship to other forms of historical evidence. Keep this in mind as you complete the following exercises.

Exercises

Exercise 1

Given the data below, interpret the pattern of crime in San Diego.

CRIMINAL CASES
IN COURT PER YEAR

1880	15
1881	24
1882	15
1883	23
1884	23
1885	31
1886	34
1887	57
1888	69
1889	70

POPULATION

City of San Diego	County of San Diego
1880: 2,637	8,618
1890: 16,159	34,987

TYPE OF CRIME	Larceny	Murder	Assault	Burglary
1880–84	6	10	24	10
1885–89	43	17	72	49

ETHNICITY	White	Hispanic	Am. Indian	Chinese	Black
1880–84	48	44	14	2	0
1885–89	207	34	12	7	1

Compiled from Richard Bigger, Metropolitan Coast: San Diego and Orange Counties, California (Los Angeles: Bureau of Governmental Research, University of California, 1958).

Perhaps a good place to start research on interpreting statistics, if you are having difficulty at this point, is Charles M. Dollar and Richard J. Jensen, *Historian's Guide to Statistics: Quantitative Analysis and Historical Research* (New York: Holt, Rinehart and Winston, Inc., 1971).

Did crime have a statistical relationship to population?

_____

By race, who were the criminally accused?

_____

How would you represent the "crime rate" to indicate that there was a Chinese "crime wave"?

_____

_____

What else would you like to know about crime statistics in this period?

_____

TO GO DEEPER:

See Steven Gottlieb, *Crime Analysis: from Concept to Reality* (Sacramento: Office of Criminal Justice Planning, 1991).

Edwin McCarthy Lemert, *The Administration of Justice to Minority Groups in Los Angeles* (Berkeley: University of California Press, 1948).

Ken Hurdle, *Confronting Violence in California* (Sacramento: Senate Publications, 1994).

Linda S. Parker, "Statutory Changes and Ethnicity in Sex Crimes in Four California Counties, 1880-1920," *Western Legal History* 6 (Winter/Spring, 1993), pp. 69-91.

Optional Exercise

Exercise 2

Given the data below, interpret the pattern of crime in San Diego County.

CONVICTION RATES IN SUPERIOR COURT BY CRIME TYPE

Native Americans

Type	Guilty	Acquitted	Dismissed	No. of Such Crimes
Assault with a Deadly Weapon	60	20	20	5
Attempted Murder	33.3	33.3	33.4	3
Grand Larceny	66.6	25	8.4	12
Murder	71.4	14.3	14.3	7

Others

Type	Guilty	Acquitted	Dismissed	No. of Such Crimes
Assault with a Deadly Weapon	50	25	25	28
Attempted Murder	37.1	11.4	51.5	35
Grand Larceny	69.2	9.3	21.5	65
Murder	35	35	30	20

From Richard W. Crawford, "White Man's Justice: Native Americans and the Judicial System of San Diego County, 1870–1890," *Western Legal History* 5 (Winter/Spring, 1992), pp. 69–81 [chart on p. 81].

Were American Indians more often found guilty of crimes than persons of other ethnic groups?

_____

How much more?

_____

Can you determine how many of the defendants were represented by counsel?

_____

_____

_____

Would that have made a difference in the verdicts? Why? How do you know that?

_____

_____

_____

_____

TO GO DEEPER:
See Clare V. McKanna Jr., "The Treatment of Indian Murderers in San Diego, 1850–1900," *Journal of San Diego History* 36 (Winter, 1990), pp. 65–77.

Optional Exercise

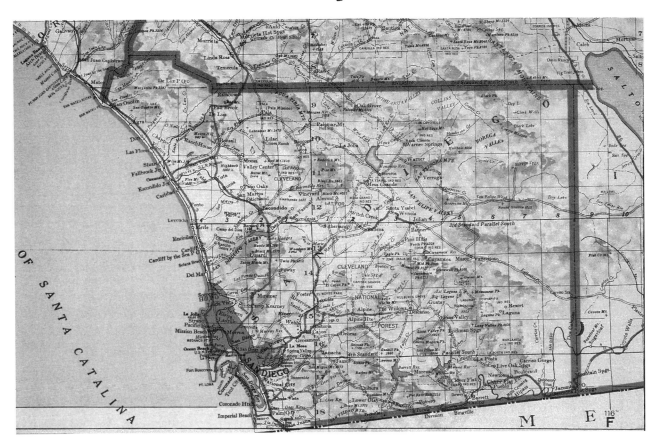

Exercise 3

Given the data below, interpret the pattern of crime in Alameda County.

CRIMINAL PROCEEDINGS IN ALAMEDA COUNTY SUPERIOR COURT, 1880–1910

Year	Felony Cases	Misdemeanors	Appeals	*Habeas Corpus*
1880–84	378	10	54	0
1885–09	350	11	39	25
1890–04	439	7	50	81
1895–09	368	4	73	77
1900–04	409	10	36	71
1905–09	687	4	34	132

From Lawrence M. Friedman and Robert V. Percival, *The Roots of Justice: Crime and Punishment in Alameda County, California, 1870–1910* (Chapel Hill: University of North Carolina Press, 1981), p. 41.

If you wanted to know if Alameda County had more crime per 1000 of population than San Diego county, what other statistic would you need?

_____

_____

What interpretation of the difference is historically sound?

_____

_____

Above: Map of San Diego, circa 1900, Heald-Henerey's geographical, commercial, and recreational map of California. Roy V. Boswell Collection for the History of Cartography, University Archives and Special Collections Section, California State University, Fullerton.

Where would you find those numbers?

_____

What is habeas corpus?

_____

Where do the cases come from on appeal to the Superior Court?

_____

Optional Exercise

TO GO DEEPER:
Read the work by Friedman and Percival mentioned in the text of this chapter to find out whether having a lawyer in a criminal proceeding changed the statistics of criminal justice.

Exercise 4

Given the data provided below, interpret the pattern of crime in Orange County.

VIOLENT CRIMES IN SELECTED JUSTICE OF THE PEACE COURTS

	Violent Crimes	Total Criminal Cases
Anaheim, 1886–1907	32	802
Fullerton/Yorba, 1897–1906	4	33
Orange, 1889–1890	2	58
Santa Ana, 1871–1888	13	184
Westminster, 1879–1898	8	84
Total	59	1,161

From John J. Stanley, "Bearers of the Burden: Justices of the Peace, Their Courts and the Law, in Orange County, California, 1870-1907," *Western Legal History* 5 (Winter/Spring, 1992), pp. 37-67 [chart on p. 67].

What percent of the total crimes handled in the justice of the peace courts were violent crimes?

_____

What was the percentage for each jurisdiction?

_____

_____

The violent crimes listed above were assault with a deadly weapon, murder, rape and assault to commit rape, and threatening to commit homicide. Does the data tell you much about how safe it was to live in any of the communities? Why?

_____

_____

_____

Based on the data and your interpretation of that data, construct a research project to determine California's pattern[s] of crime in the period, 1850–1910. In describing your project, you should include the types of data desirable for the project, where you might find that data, and a series of questions about the data that would be most useful for analysis.

_____

_____

_____

_____

_____

_____

_____

_____

_____

Exercise 5

Read the following newspaper stories about a murder trial in Orange County and take notes about what aspects of this case might be quantified. In other words, as you read the following documents you should continue to ask yourself How many? For example: How many days did the trial take? How many attorneys were involved in the proceedings? How many witnesses were called to the stand? You also could ask questions beyond the contents of the story. How many women were accused of crime in the 1890s? Of those, how many were convicted? Remember, quantification asks about quantity. After you have collected that quantifiable information, it is time to start asking analytic questions.

Los Angeles Times, December 19, 1899

TRIAL OF MRS. COOK BEGUN

The trial of Mrs. Katie Cook, for shooting and killing her husband, T. J. Cook, August 20, was begun in the Superior Court today [Dec. 18]. Since the tragedy Mrs. Cook has been suffering greatly from nervous prostration, but has so far recovered now as to sit composedly in the prisoner's dock between her father and mother, who will remain with her throughout the trial. Mrs. Cook has admitted the killing of her husband by shooting him through the head while he lay sleeping on a couch near her bed.

It had been an open secret for some time that Cook's association with other women was notorious, and when this became so bad that his wife could stand it no longer, and after being threatened with death if she exposed him, she took the law into her own hands, sending a bullet through his brain as he lay sleeping on a mattress by the side of her own bed, after returning, it is alleged by Mrs. Cook, from the room occupied by their hired girl. Cook had been a notorious character for the past several years. He had been mixed up in several shooting scrapes, only last year shooting and killing Jasper Grigsby in a quarrel on the public highway in the peatlands. A few years ago he quarreled with his brother, both men emptying their guns at one another without effect. Public sympathy is strongly with Mrs. Cook.

Los Angeles Times, December 20, 1899

SECOND DAY OF THE TRIAL

OF MRS. KATIE COOK

The second day of the trial of Mrs. Katie Cook for the killing of her husband, T.J. Cook, was attended by many spectators from all over the county. Mrs. Cook, accompanied by her father, mother and brother, entered the courtroom just as the bailiff announced the opening of court, and took a chair immediately behind her attorneys. Mrs. Cook apparently pays but little attention to the details of the trial.

The jury was completed by noon and this afternoon the prosecution called the first witness, W. W. Barton. He was a hired man in the Cook family and was the first person to see Cook after he had been shot by his wife. Barton's testimony was substantially the same as at the preliminary examination. He told of his being awakened about 4 o'clock on the morning of August 28 by a pistol shot, followed by a commotion and loud talking in an adjoining room, occupied by Mabel Moody, the hired girl. Upon entering the room he said Mrs. Cook was flourishing a smoking pistol and talking very excitedly to Miss Moody, accusing her of taking her husband. In addition to his testimony at the preliminary trial, Barton testified that on the previous evening, while Cook was trimming Miss Moody's finger nails, Mrs. Cook left the room with tears in her eyes, going upstairs to her room; that he soon went to his room, leaving Cook and Miss Moody alone; that about 11 o'clock he heard some one walk into Miss Moody's room, and afterward heard two voices, those of a man and woman; that when he entered Miss Moody's room a few minutes after the pistol shot next morning he noticed by the pillows and the appearance of the bed that it had been occupied by more than one person.

Deputy Sheriff Bush testified as to a conversation with Mrs. Cook a few hours after the shooting; that she told him Cook had gone to live with the Moody girl one week before the previous night and that since that time he had been sleeping on a couch in their room near a door leading to Miss Moody's room. George McPhee, a reporter, testified to practically the same facts, with the addition that Mrs. Cook's condition was apparently that of a distracted woman, and she seemed not accountable for what she was doing.

George W. More, a neighbor, testified as to receiving the revolver with which the shooting was done and identified the same. Henry Pope, father of Mrs. Cook, was put upon the stand and questioned relative to the search of Cook's papers for an alleged deed to the valuable peatland farm of the deceased from Mrs. Cook to her husband, but he testified that the same had not been found. The prosecution then introduced J.A. Turner, a notary public, to prove that such a deed had been acknowledged. Objection was made, and pending argument on this point, court adjourned until tomorrow. The defense is making a strong fight to not permit this evidence at the present stage of the trial, as it will tend to strengthen the theory that Mrs. Cook had another motive than that of injured feelings for killing her husband. Interest increases as the trial progresses, the courtroom not being large enough to accommodate half the spectators.

Los Angeles Times, December 21, 1899

COOK MURDER TRIAL

NEARING AN END

A large crowd was again in attendance at the Cook murder trial today. Mrs. Cook still retains that stolid indifference which has characterized her conduct since the beginning of her trial. She appears to notice nothing in particular, taking apparently no interest whatever in what is going on around her. She enters the courtroom with her father, mother, and brother, and sits with them calmly until adjournment. But once today did her demeanor change, and that was when Mabel Moody, the hired girl, was called from the witness room to the stand. At the mention of her name by Attorney Davis, Mrs. Cook started. She moved nervously in her chair, and as the girl was conducted in front of her by a Deputy Sheriff, her face assumed a crimson hue. Soon regaining her composure, however, she took but little interest in what the girl said.

Miss Moody had been called by the defense, the prosecution having rested after succeeding in getting evidence admitted relative to the acknowledgement of a deed to the Cook ranch made by Mrs. Cook to her husband a few weeks previous to his death. Her evidence related principally to the apparent mental condition of Mrs. Cook for two weeks previous to Cook's death, and was in effect that she was not responsible for what she did. For several days she had taken little or no interest in household affairs. She seemed depressed, absent-minded and weak, and the greater portion of her time was spent lying on a couch, crying hysterically. The question whether or not, in her judgment, Mrs. Cook during that time knew right from wrong, asked by Attorney Davis, brought out vehement objections from counsel for the people. Heated debate followed, lasting more than an hour, during which many authorities were cited. The court finally admitting the question, the girl answered that she thought she did not. Miss Moody was not questioned, either in direct or cross-examination, as to whether Cook entered her room on the night of the killing.

The only other witness examined was J.H. Paty, a butcher, who visited the Cook home two or three times each week. His evidence tended to show a steady decline in Mrs. Cook for several weeks previous to the tragedy. In his judgment she had become daft for some reason, he knew not what. Upon the conclusion of Paty's evidence, court adjourned until tomorrow.

Los Angeles Times, Dec. 22, 1899

BAD REPUTATION OF TOM COOK

AIRED IN COURT

For years Tom Cook has been known here by many people as a very immoral man, but until today the full import of his hellish disposition was not realized. Mrs. Cook has been severely criticised by some people for taking the law into her own hands, but not by the spectators who today heard the evidence of twenty-six witnesses as to Cook's reputation for chastity. Neighbors east, west, north and south of Cook's ranch home testified that they would not themselves permit their wives to go to his house on account of his bad reputation. Residents of Santa Ana testified that while Cook lived here several years ago women of questionable reputation visited his home at almost all hours of the day and night. Five young girls, one of whom is but 15, testified that Cook had attempted to take improper liberties with them while they were the guests of Mrs. Cook.

One girl testified that while she was visiting Mrs. Cook, her husband compelled both herself and his wife to sit and listen while he read them over twenty pages of a vulgar poetical effusion, declaring he would kill them both if they did not listen to it, or if they ever told on him. All the witnesses today testified that the reputation of Mrs. Cook for chastity and purity of character was of the very best. Many also testified as to threats made by Cook to kill his wife if she left him or told of his immoral practices. Mrs. Graham, wife of Jailer Graham, testified as to Mrs. Cook's condition when she was brought to the jail the next day after she had killed her husband; that her mind seemed almost gone; that she was very thin in flesh, extremely nervous and hysterical, and that she begged not to be left alone. After she was released on bail she preferred to stay at the jail, which she did for several weeks. It was with considerable difficulty for weeks after the tragedy that she could be persuaded to take sufficient nourishment to keep her alive.

The case was not postponed today until Saturday as was expected, Judge Ballard announcing that he had postponed the law and motion business, thus giving an opportunity for this case to be concluded this week. Attorneys for the defense stated tonight they will conclude their case early tomorrow. The case will probably go to the jury Saturday evening.

Los Angeles Times, December 23, 1899

TESTIMONY OF MRS. COOK

IN HER OWN BEHALF TAKEN

Tension was high today when Mrs. Cook was put on the stand in her own behalf, the courtroom rapidly filling up until standing room was at a premium, and the crowd extending out into the hall and down the stairway upon the street. Court convened half an hour earlier this morning, so as to get through with the case, if possible, before Christmas. The first several witnesses testified as to Mrs. Cook's apparent mental condition preceding the tragedy.

W. W. Baston, Cook's hired man, testified that upon several occasions previous to the tragedy, Mrs. Cook imagined that a woman was after her with a pistol, trying to kill her. Upon one occasion, she came running into the house just at dark, screaming that a woman was in the barn with a pistol, and was trying to shoot her, and it took the combined efforts of Cook and himself to persuade her to accompany them to the barn to prove to her that no one was there. He also testified that the greater portion of the time she was crying. Another time, while working near the house with Cook, they saw Mrs. Cook come from an upstairs window out upon the roof of the porch, wringing her hands and crying, that Cook hurried to the house, going through the front door and upstairs, that meanwhile Mrs. Cook was kneeling at the edge of the roof with her hands clasped as if in the act of prayer, and that just as she arose and stepped back, Cook rushed through the window grabbing her before she could hurl herself off.

But the court, jury and the great crowd of spectators were apparently moved when Mrs. Cook took the stand, and in answer to questions from Attorney Davis, told of the unspeakable life led by her husband, and how, from threats, she feared to expose him. Slowly and in a low tone of voice, she told how he had brought young girls to their home, and how he had accomplished their ruin; how she had entreated him to live different; how she had begged him to send the girls away; how he had cursed her and sworn he would kill her if she ever exposed him; how she knew full well he would make his threats good; how he compelled one German servant girl to appear in the "all-together" before himself and Mrs. Cook; how he compelled another young girl and herself to sit and listen to the reading of page after page of the vilest poetry known to the tenderloin district; how he openly boasted to her of his degradation, and what he would do with her if she betrayed him.

Question after question from Mr. Davis brought her down to within a few weeks before the tragedy. Then she told of Mabel Moody's coming to live with them; how Cook left her bed and boasted of it; how, at times she thought she would die; how, the night before his death, Cook sat down in the sitting-room trimming Miss Moody's finger nails, and the language he used, how she left the room and went into the kitchen, where she wept bitterly; how she went up stairs to her room; how Cook came later, and how she implored him to leave the girl and live with her; how he refused, and lay down on his bed near the door through a closet leading to Miss Moody's room; how, about 11 o'clock, he left his bed, going into the girl's room; how he stayed there until about 2 o'clock in the morning; how, when he returned, she went to his couch in her night attire, and kneeling by him, again implored him to come and live with her, be true to her, and to forsake his wicked ways; how he pushed her away—and then she knew no more.

From that time until the following week, when her brother, who had not spoken to her from the day she married Cook, until he called her by name in the County Jail, her mind has been a blank. She remembers nothing that transpired during that time. Tom Cook was "dead" with a bullet hole between his eyes, lying on his couch in apparent peaceful repose, the next morning after he had visited Mable Moody's room on the night of August 27, and many residents of the peatland district breathed easier, for he was a dangerous man with a gun.

Mrs. Cook stood the trying ordeal of relating all this misery remarkably well, until she came to where she was kneeling at his side and importing him to return to her. Then she burst into tears, sobbing bitterly for some minutes, during which many handkerchiefs throughout the courtroom brushed away tears. At this juncture the court asked Attorney Davis to delay questioning the witness further until another small court matter could be attended to. . . . Court then adjourned until tomorrow, when it is expected the case will be submitted to the jury.

Los Angeles Times, December 24, 1899

MRS. COOK QUICKLY

ACQUITTED OF CHARGE OF MURDER

Mrs. Cook was acquitted this evening of the charge of murder in less than fifteen minutes. There was the greatest demonstration ever witnessed in the courtroom here when the verdict became known. Upon the jurymen filing into the box, and being polled by the clerk, Judge Ballard said: "Gentlemen, have you arrived upon a verdict?" "We have," answered the foreman. "What is your verdict?" asked the judge. At this juncture Mrs. Cook, who up to this time had been apparently indifferent as to her surroundings, leaned forward anxiously in her chair and faced the jury box. "Not guilty," spoke the foreman. Mrs. Cook fell into the arms of her mother, and the great crowd of spectators arose as one person, filling the corridors with deafening applause. Such a scene probably never was witnessed in the courtroom before. One juryman remarked after the adjournment of court, that he was sorry the jury could not have awarded a medal to Mrs. Cook.

Before adjourning yesterday the defense introduced expert medical testimony on the sanity of Mrs. Cook. Four physicians, J. M. Lacy, C.D. Ball, W. H. Hill, and C. F. Bruner, testified that she was evidently insane at the time she killed her husband. Two other witnesses were introduced to prove that she had received two hard falls, striking on her head, while driving from this city out to her home. This was about three years ago. This morning the defense rested, and the argument of the attorneys before the jury began, Attorney Jud Rush of Los Angeles making one of the best addresses before a jury that has ever been heard in the county. He was followed by Victor Montgomery of this city, for the defense. Attorney Jackson speaking for the prosecution. Then came Lecomte Davis of Los Angeles, whose picture of the depravity of the murdered man was vehement, while the recital of the misery of the trusting wife pathetic. The jury was apparently moved by Davis's characteristic address. District Atty. Williams closed the argument. Judge Ballard following with a brief but vigorous charge to the jury.

Lists of Quantifiable facts. (If you run out of room, you may wish to continue your lists on separate pieces of paper.)

Note: If in doubt, refer back to the preface to these documents for some hints.

_____

_____

_____

_____

_____

_____

_____

_____

Name _____   Instructor _____   Date _____

_____

_____

_____

_____

_____

_____

_____

_____

_____

_____

_____

_____

_____

TO GO DEEPER:

Read the following secondary sources to help you put the Cook trial in context and for help in identifying possible research topics.

Shelley Bookspan, *A Germ of Goodness: The California State Prison System, 1851–1944* (Lincoln: University of Nebraska Press, 1991).

Mary E. Odem, *Delinquent Daughters: Protecting and Policing Adolescent Female Sexuality in the United States, 1885 to 1920* (Chapel Hill: University of North Carolina Press, 1995).

Joycelyn M. Pollock-Burne, *Women, Prison and Crime* (Pacific Grove: Brooks/Cole Publishing, 1990).

Women waited until 1917 to get access to jury service. See Odem, *Delinquent Daughters*, p. 74.

Optional Exercise

Name _____   **Instructor** _____   **Date** _____

Locating and Assessing Sources

Armed with a topic and a general reading knowledge of your subject, you are ready to conduct research of your own in order to write a paper. Libraries are the most important place to start. As you probably are well aware, most libraries list all of their holdings electronically on OPAC (Online Public Access Catalog); those institutions unable to computerize still have card catalogues. All libraries, however, are staffed by professionals trained to assist you. Local historical societies are less likely to offer computer-assisted search systems, but they are very likely to offer the services of knowledgeable personnel willing to help you find and work with primary sources.

Begin your search for useful sources—books periodicals, government documents, audiovisual material—in your school's library. If you have a computer in your home or dormitory, you may be able to access OPAC via modem. (Of course, you still have to go the library to access the materials you want to see.) In OPAC, titles are arranged not only under the traditional card-catalog categories of Author, Title, and Subject but also under Title Words and Keywords. In the latter two categories you do not need to know the acceptable subject headings before you begin your search.

Say your instructor has already suggested a number of works on your research topic that you should consult. To search online for these works by title press "T" and then keyboard in the title you wish to find. If the bibliographic information for the title and its call number come up, press "S" to see any similar items. Hopefully, the screen will now fill up with information on related sources, fixing a body of literature for you to consult. Searching for works by an author is just as simple, but remember to list the author's last name first, followed by a comma, one space, and the author's first name. To search by subject, often the best way to find useful materials if you are beginning your search without a recommended reading list, start by pressing "S" and then keyboard in the subject you want to search. Because OPAC uses a controlled vocabulary when searching by subject, you might want to refer to the *Library of Congress Subject Heading Books* (located in your library's reference section) to determine those control words. Examples of valid subject headings include "California History 1850–1950" and "Divorce California."

A deeper level of research may be conducted in FirstSearch, a computerized system of databases including World Cat. FirstSearch is the umbrella name for a service that markets WorldCat. FirstSearch has approximately 80 other databases. World Cat is a catalog containing 36 million books, periodicals, government documents, etc., owned by libraries worldwide. Once you have located a title by any means, check to see whether your library owns a copy; if not, you need to work with the interlibrary loan librarian to obtain one. FirstSearch also contains an Articles search database; its listings, however, are largely limited to twentieth-century material. Again, once you have identified the author, title, periodical title, volume, date, and page numbers for an article you wish to consult, check the periodical section of your library before requesting the assistance of the interlibrary-loan librarian.

Be certain to visit the reference section of the library. There you will find two useful guides. The first one is the *Directory of Archival and Manuscript Repositories in California* published by the Society of California Archivists in 1984. This guide will help identify local sites for your research. Second, of similar significance, is Margaret Miller Rocq's *California Local History: A Local Bibliography and Union List of Library Holdings* (1970), which will help you sharpen your objectives when visiting a local library or historical society. Please note that all such reference works are dated and most libraries and historical societies regularly acquire manuscript collections. You will need the assistance of the professional personnel at the local facility to learn of any recent acquisitions in your research field.

There may be some other very exciting services available to you in the reference room. *America: History and Life* (Santa Barbara: ABC-Clio, 1954-) is a guide to periodical literature, books, book reviews, and doctoral dissertations in history. It is available in print and on CD-ROM. If your library has the hard copy only, fine. But if it owns the CD-ROM version, you will find it much easier to use. The *Humanities Index* (New York: H. W. Wilson, 1975-) lists articles from over 300 scholarly periodicals. Again, a CD-ROM version may be available in your library. The *Social Sciences Index* (New York: H. W. Wilson, 1975-) lists articles from 350 periodicals in disciplines including economics, geography, and political science. This is an important index to use in conjunction with history resources.

Now that you have identified secondary sources, you need to start taking notes. For each "hit" you make on the computer screen—as well as for each source you manage to identify the old fashioned way—you need to create a note card. We recommend using 5 x 8 cards because you probably will need a good deal of space in which to take useful notes. If you are able to download bibliographic information off the computer system you are using, retain that information on a disk and a print out a hard copy for use later in the stacks (as well as for security should something happen to your computer file). The advantage of taking the time to prepare note cards even at this early stage in your research is bibliographic as well as categorical. For example, one hit for the subject search "California History 1850–1950" is *Practicing Law in Frontier California.* On the back of the card, record the source's bibliographic information:

> Gordon Morris Bakken, *Practicing Law in Frontier California* (Lincoln: University of Nebraska Press, 1991).

The reason for doing this revolves around one of the most basic assumptions about history: when presenting your research in written form, you must be able to document the sources you consulted to build your evidence and form your interpretation. The computer will tell you only that the book contains information on the practice of law and lawyers in California. Now it's time to go to the source, in this case the library stacks. Picking the book off the library shelf and simply scanning its table of contents and index will reveal that it contains information on topics including debt collection, tort, corporations, criminal law, and public image. Reference to the chapter on criminal law discloses material on vigilantism, including a revisionist interpretation of the phenomenon. Now use the front of the card to record the topical contents of this secondary source. Depending on your research objectives, be certain to include in your descrip-tions at least three pertinent key words (which you may want to highlight—or boldface—for easy identification later). Later, when you sort your cards (be they paper cards or word-processing files) by topic, the wisdom of early and extensive classification will become abundantly clear. Another good thing about actually getting your hands on the sources is this: even if the book you pull down from the shelf turns out not to be useful to your research, you will be surprised by how much you will have learned by browsing through it. Certainly computer search engines are powerful tools, but there is no substitute for visiting the sources firsthand.

Once you have familiarized yourself with the secondary texts on your subject, which, as you know, is necessary to establish a context for your subject, it is time to track down the primary documents, often the most fruitful sources. Again, when handling primary sources—whether considering them firsthand, on microfilm, or via the World Wide Web—take the time to keep good bibliographical and topical notations: don't spare the note cards! Here you may well ask: How do I assess a primary document in order to extract useful bibliographic and topical data? It is easy to do so when considering a secondary source, but categorizing primary sources takes a bit of practice.

Let's say on microfilm you find an editorial in the January 24, 1850, edition of the *Daily Alta California.* The editorial attacks "incendiarism in San Francisco" calling it "more heinous than any other deliberate murder." The editorial goes on to say that "merchants must organize a system of private watchmen" and that a fire department is needed to guard against arsonists.

First, capture the citation: *Daily Alta California,* Jan. 24, 1850. Note the place of publication: **San Francisco.** Then, identify the largest issue, the topic: **Crime.** What is the subtopic? "Incendiarism." But what is that? Be certain you know the definition of the term . . . **Arson**, then record it as the subtopic. Is there another subtopic? What about the proposed organization of merchants and a fire department? Depending on the breadth of your search, both could be subtopics. Now record on the note card certain words and phrases that you may wish to quote in your paper; enclose these in quotation marks. Finally, record your own thoughts about the possible meaning of the evidence you have just uncovered. Now that you have the hang of it, practice taking useful notes on the many excerpted primary sources that follow. Remember, your topic and subtopic selections are useful for sorting note cards after your research is concluded. When it comes time to start writing, your carefully prepared note cards will be a great asset. We promise.

Exercises

Exercise 1

Create note cards for the following:

1. Editorial entitled "Ruffianism" in the Dec. 30, 1850 edition of the *Daily California Alta*

"Assaults and robberies are matters of nightly occurrence and it is most evident the city is infected with some of the worst scoundrels in Christendom. Where they have been arrested they are proven to be immigrants from the penal colonies of Great Britain."

Citation:

_____

Place:

_____

Topic:

_____

Subtopic:

_____

Subtopic:

_____

Quotation/Meaning:

_____

_____

2. *Daily Alta California,* February 24, 1851

The Courts and the People

There can be no doubt that 500 murders have been committed in California . . . not one single offender has been punished by these courts. Every murderer who has passed through trial has been let loose . . . .

Citation:

_____

Place:

_____

Topic:

_____

Subtopic:

_____

Quotation/Meaning:

_____

_____

3. *Los Angeles Star,* May 24, 1851
"Thieves"
   On Sunday night last, five horses were stolen from Mr. Lathrop's corral. On the same night a valuable horse was stolen from Wm. Carey Jones, Esq. Judge Lynch's shop was broke open, and a pistol and a quantity of mechanic's tools stolen. In the absence of an efficient police, our citizens must take measures to protect their property.

Citation:

_____

Place:

_____

Topic:

_____

Subtopic:

_____

Quotation/Meaning:

_____

_____

4. *Los Angeles Star,* May 24, 1851
Incendiaries seem to abound in San Francisco
   "...An attempt was made last week to set fire to the City Hospital but the diabolical plot was not successful. Three cheers for the men who will hang the scoundrels..."

Citation:

_____

Copyright © 1999 Harlan Davidson, Inc.

Name   **Instructor**   **Date**

Place:
Note: is this story about Los Angeles, the place of publication, or San Francisco? Think about this carefully before settling on an answer.

_____

Topic:

_____

Subtopic:

_____

Quotation/Meaning:

_____

_____

_____

5. *Los Angeles Star,* May 24, 1851
A Mob Hanging in Napa
". . . The criminally accused. McCauley, was convicted of murdering "Judge Sellers" and was sentenced to hang on Friday, May 16. The Governor arrived and commuted the sentence to life imprisonment. Upon hearing of the Governor's action, a large group of "Napa Citizens" gathers and "proceeded to the cell of McCauley, and cooly and deliberately hung him up to a beam, where the body was found the next morning."

Citation:

_____

Place:

_____

Topic:

_____

Subtopic:

_____

Quotation/Meaning:

_____

6. *From a letter from William Higby to his father, dated June 12, 1851, from San Francisco*

"The People have become dissatisfied with the public authorities of the city because criminals are not brought to justice and punished as their deeds merit." [However, Higby provides a long description of a burglar caught in the act about 9 P.M., brought to trial that day, convicted and sentenced to death at midnight, and executed at 2:30 A.M. He observed that the event was] "a fearful retribution inflicted by an indignant and outraged people."

Note: Because this is the first letter you have encountered, we will help you out a bit on this one.

Citation: William Higby to Father, June 12, 1851, William Higby Collection, MSS, California State Library, Sacramento, Box 218.

The first part of the citation indicates the nature of the document, its date, and the name of the collection. The MSS indicates that the source is a manuscript primary source, not a printed primary source. The California State Library is the institution that holds the letter. Sacramento is the location of the Library and Box 218 is the manuscript box that houses the letter.

Place: San Francisco.

This is on the face of the letter, and the author is observing the events in San Francisco. A reading of letters by other authors and newspaper stories written in June 1851 further authenticates the place of observation as well as the nature of the events.

Topic:

_____

Subtopic:

_____

Quotation/Meaning:

_____

_____

7. *Los Angeles Star,* August 9, 1851

Governor's Proclamation Concerning Vigilance Committees

"Our government is a government of laws, and that though they may sometimes prove inadequate, sometimes operate oppressively, or be administered corruptly, the remedy is not in a destruction of the entire system, but is to be secured by a peaceful resort to those constitutional means which are wisely afforded to reform whatever abuse may exist and correct whatever errors may have been committed."

Citation:

_____

Place:

_____

Topic:

_____

Subtopic:

_____

Quotation/Meaning:

_____

_____

_____

8. *From a letter of John Hume to Jane Hume Williams, dated April 18, 1852, from Placerville, in the James B. Hume Collection in the Bancroft Library, Berkeley, California.*

    "The constant excitement of life here is wearing and tiresome, and the country is full of crime and bloody tragedies. Within the past week two men were hung for stealing by a mob at Coloma. . . . Today I have obtained warrants for two men, on a charge of larceny, and when I close this letter shall go straight to a Justice office to prosecute them."

Citation:

_____

Place:

_____

Topic:

_____

Subtopic:

_____

Quotation/Meaning:

_____

_____

9. Los Angeles Star, July 16, 1853

An Insurrection

"...This county is in a state of insurrection, clearly and plainly so. A large gang of outlaws, many of them expelled for crimes from the mines, are in open rebellion against the laws, and are daily committing the most daring murders and robberies. One of two things must result: the orderly, industrious inhabitants must drive out this worthless scum of humanity, or they must give way before the pirates and be driven out themselves. . . . Let good citizens combine and drive the rascals headlong into the sea."

Citation:

_____

Place:

_____

Topic:

_____

Subtopic:

_____

Quotation/Meaning:

_____

_____

10. *Los Angeles Star,* September 20, 1853 in the Adams and Company (San Francisco) Scrapbook, volume 2, page 26 at the Huntington Library, San Marino, California

Outrage and Prompt Punishment

"On Wednesday an attempt was made by a Californian, named Isidro Albitro, to commit a rape upon the person of Mrs. Margarita Temple, wife of Francisco Temple, in her own house, and at midday, at the Puente. . . . On Thursday, a detachment of the rangers and many of our most substantial citizens, went out to examine the case, and, if necessary, to inflict such punishment as would serve as a warning to all such men, disposed to violate the sanctity of domestic life.

The meeting was called to order by Judge Scott and Samuel Arbuckle, Esq., appointed Chairman, and Hon. S.C. Foster, Secretary. Messrs D.W. Alexander, John Reid and Andres Pico were appointed a committee to nominate a jury of twelve men, to hear the evidence and decide the fate of the prisoner. This jury found the accused guilty and recommended "250 lashes on the bare back; that he have his head cropped, and leave the county as soon as his physicians pronounce him able to do so. And that if he be again found in the county that he be hung."

The sentence was approved by the meeting, and ordered to be carried into effect. The punishment was inflicted. . . ."

Citation:

_____

Place:

_____

Topic:

_____

Subtopic:

_____

Quotation/Meaning:

_____

_____

_____

11. *San Francisco Daily Herald,* March 27, 1854 in the Adams and Company Scrapbook, volume 3, page 107, Huntington Library

[A horse thief named Schwartz met his maker at the end of a rope and Judge Eno has issued warrants for the arrest of all the parties concerned in this outrage.]

"The horse was the property of Evans, White & Co. of that place. It was stolen on the 15th inst., and traced to the ranch of the thief, on the Yuba river, where he was taken, and the horse recovered. The man was brought to Jackson at a very early hour this morning, and immediately hung, without the ceremony of a trial. There was no doubt of his guilt, which is the only justification for the deed."

Citation:

_____

Place:

_____

Topic:

_____

Subtopic:

_____

Quotation/Meaning:

_____

_____

Name _____   **Instructor** _____   **Date** _____

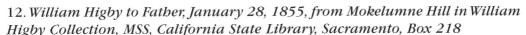

12. *William Higby to Father, January 28, 1855, from Mokelumne Hill in William Higby Collection, MSS, California State Library, Sacramento, Box 218*

"Criminal offences are attended to as soon as heard of. I do not hesitate, day or night, week day or Sunday; I am always ready to act to such cases and leave no room for escape. It is necessary here to attend at the moment, people move so much. I do so that people may have confidence in the authorities and to avoid or keep down mob law or lynching. I think our county is as free from mob law as any other county in the state.

One thing has encouraged lynching more of late. Our Governor has commuted the punishment of several under sentence of death to imprisonment. Much dissatisfaction has been caused by it."

Citation:

_____

Place: (Be certain to list the county and its location in the state.)

_____

Topic:

_____

Subtopic:

_____

Quotation/Meaning:

_____

_____

Mokelumne Hill. Courtesy of the California History Room, California State Library, Sacramento, California.

Name   Instructor   Date

13. *San Francisco Daily Herald,* November 8, 1855, in Adams and Company Scrapbook, vol. 5, pp. 150–1, Huntington Library.

[Filipe Espinosa was accused of attempting to rape a six year old child. The child identified him as the assailant.]

"His Honor, Judge Freelon, remarked that the prisoner might not be convicted of an attempt to commit rape, but the Court had reason for the horrible suspicion that many Mexican boys and men employed about families, without being so foolish as to attempt to commit rape on children of such tender age, were in the habit of tampering with their bodies so as to excite their lust and gratify it by self pollution. . . . It appears that horrors of the most unnatural description are being accumulated on this singular trial. . . . Several jurors, however, confessed to a confusion of recollection as to the date assigned to the commission of the offense, and the mother was recalled to the stand, and testified that the day when she was told by the child of the attempt upon her person was the same on which the prisoner proved an alibi by Mexican testimony. The mother testified at the same time that the child had told her of other similar attempts made by the prisoner; but the proof of an alibi was confined to the date of the single particular offence charged in the indictment. The jury acquitted the prisoner."

Citation:

_____

Place:

_____

Topic:

_____

Subtopic:

_____

Quotation/Meaning:

_____

_____

14. *Los Angeles Star,* March 1, 1856 (A story about Jose Buenavedez and a hung jury in his robbery case.)

We regret that there are many such graceless villains in our midst that have long evaded their just deserts, and if there is any virtue in a rope's end, we would like to see it generously administered to all such cases, and thereby relieve the county of an onerous bill of expense.

Citation:

_____

Place:

_____

Topic:

_____

Subtopic:

_____

Quotation/Meaning:

_____

_____

15. *Daily Alta California,* March 2, 1857
Heavy Fine-Inequity
(A story regarding a $500 fine levied upon 12 Chinese for gambling.)
[Such a fine against such] "poor, ignorant, inoffensive persons" [seemed unfair when compared to fines against white men of not more] "than $100."

Citation:

_____

Place:

_____

Topic:

_____

Subtopic:

_____

Quotation/Meaning:

_____

_____

16. *Los Angeles Star,* December 4, 1858
(A story about Pancho Daniel objecting to the failure to give him a fair trial.)
"If we are to be governed by laws erected under the constitution, then let action of those laws be general. Let there not be statute law for one man and lynch law for another. If we are to have anarchy and confusion prevail, let the announcement be made, so that all may have warning."

Name   Instructor   Date

Citation:

_____

Place:

_____

Topic:

_____

Subtopic:

_____

Quotation/Meaning:

_____

_____

17. *Los Angeles Star,* January 8, 1859
    (A story about C. W. Moore shooting Nieves Perez on Jan. 3.)
    "There is an impression that one class of citizens may commit any outrage on another class without impunity; we wish to see all such feeling done away with."

Citation:

_____

Place:

_____

Topic:

_____

Subtopic:

_____

Quotation/Meaning:

_____

_____

18. *Contra Costa County Gazette,* April 26, 1862
    "The practice of stealing and selling young Indians, seems to have become quite common in some parts of our State. Even cruelty is added to the crime. . . .

Old Indians are even murdered in order to secure their children. The men engaged in this business go stealthily at night into the Indian camps, and carry off, by force, the little ones, while all are asleep. If detected in the act, the knife or revolver protects them. In this way says the Mendocino Herald, from which this statement is derived, there "have doubtless been sacrificed hundreds of Indians in this and adjoining counties within the last year or two, and no doubt, much of the hostile feeling ingendered by the Diggers towards the Whites, is thus engendered, and is aggravated from time to time by new acts of aggression. Many of the depradations committed by them, too, are the legitimate result of retaliation for friends and clansmen thus murdered or forcibly carried off."

A California Maidu woman using a traditional seed beater. Courtesy The Field Museum, #1835, Chicago.

Citation:

_____

Place:

_____

Topic:

_____

Subtopic:

_____

Quotation/Meaning:

_____

_____

19. *Contra Costa County Gazette,* August 6, 1870

The Maggie Ryan Murder

"The trial of Quin for the murder of the child, Maggie Ryan, in January last is now being conducted before Judge Dwinelle in the 15th District Court for the city and county of San Francisco, the defense, apparently, being only that the prisoner is an idiot and brute, and not responsible for indulgence of brutal propensities. It must be that the prisoner has but few human attributes, but the plea of the defense, if allowed, would give a fearful license to brutality."

Name   Instructor   Date

Citation:

_____

Place:

_____

Topic:

_____

Subtopic:

_____

Quotation/Meaning:

_____

_____

20. *The Mariposa Gazette,* September 1, 1877
The Jury System

"The jury system is a magnificent system: we believe it is called by some idiotic people the bulwark of freedom; the palladium of liberty. Before a jury of one's peers are brought cases for adjudication, upon the result of which may depend life, liberty, property interests, reputation, future character and social standing. The San Francisco *Spirit of the Times* of August 25th, in an able editorial on this subject, very appropriately asks: What does a jury of one's peers mean? We have long desired to know; will not some learned pundit inform us? We had the pleasure of looking upon twelve "good and true" men, a short time since, who were called upon to weigh and consider the nicest law points; to well and truly try, upon the testimony adduced, questions at issue, weighty and important; and to render a verdict in accordance with their ideas of the legal propositions adduced. We have nothing to urge against that jury, but we say now, without the fear of contradiction, that they *couldn't* decide in accordance with their ideas as to the difference between right and wrong; for the simple reason, they had no ideas. They were as solid, ignorant, unintellectual, dull and stupid a looking body as could be found anywhere. Not a single gleam of intelligence shot from their eyes. When the counsel engaged discussed law questions, of great interest even to a lawman, and made interesting points, which excited the greatest attention from the court, counsel, parties at interest and audience; these "peers" sitting in the jury box, paid about as much attention to what was transpiring as the fat boy in Picwick. What a reflection upon the parties interested in the case being tried; to call such men their "peers." For as a sequence, if these men are "peers," then the parties involved, have within them the concentrated essence of everything assinine [sic]. It is a disgrace from beginning to end that so little care should be taken securing the right kind of jurors to sit upon important cases. Why, were our life in danger, and such a jury as that by which we illustrate, was called upon to give decision as to our future "long life and happiness," we would save any trouble in the matter, and like the coon when Captain Scott pulled trigger on him, would come down, acknowledge the corn, and calmly, and with resignation enter his game bag. What a farce to talk of the right and justice of the decision of a jury, when a portion of the body cannot read nor write; and when one of them, endeavoring to get through his head, the nature of the discussion between counsel as to the exhaustion of challenges, was under the impression a warm argument was going on as to the price of cheese. It is monstrous that such things should be allowed. We would rather submit any question at issue, which required the application of legal provisions to solve and settle, to a fair minded Judge in the quietude of his Chambers, than to a jury of "peers," unless we could personally select them-not with any regard to the merits of the case, but entirely to the fact of their intelligence. As the jury system is operated and carried out at the present time, it is a farce in the broadest sense of the word. No jury of one's peers, at least not to our way of thinking."

Citation:

_____

Place:

_____

Topic:

_____

Subtopic:

_____

Quotation/Meaning:

_____

_____

21. *The Weekly Delta* [Visalia], February 7, 1879
Massacre in Mariposa
"A most atrocious and bloody deed was perpetrated by citizens of Mariposa county on a camp of defenseless Indians, a few days ago. The trouble appears to have originated for a settled belief, that Indians were to blame for certain murders that had been committed there within the past two or three years. A party of men known as the "Chowchilla rangers" visited an Indian camp occupied by six men and one squaw, in the night. These men—E. G. Laird, Robert Laird, Samuel Laird, Fred Holt, John Hale, Nat. Green,—Bebdricks and one other, took out an old man, hung him and fired several shots into his body before he was dead. They also killed three young men shooting them all in the head. They also wounded the squaw severely. Two of the Indians made their escape to Mariposa, and gave the news. The officers started in pursuit immediately and at latest advices had succeeded in capturing four of the party, among them E. G. Laird, the ring leader of the gang."

Citation:

_____

Place:

_____

Topic:

_____

Subtopic:

_____

Quotation/Meaning:

_____

_____

22. *Contra Costa County Gazette,* January 10, 1880

"We are sorry that Governor Irwin should have blemished the admirable record of his administration, just as he was about closing it, by pardoning from the State Prison, Morgan, the notorious poll tax forger, who plundered the State and county revenues of San Francisco so extensively and successfully, and who has never surrendered any of his ill-gotten gains, or recompensed the State in any way for his crime. On the contrary, he is reported to have enjoyed extraordinary privileges during his convict term, rather to the provocation of discontent among convicts subjected to the strict rules of prison discipline."

Citation:

_____

Place:

_____

Topic:

_____

Subtopic:

_____

Quotation/Meaning:

_____

_____

23. *Contra Costa County Gazette,* April 17, 1880

Dirty Dog

"A tramp was arrested at the railroad depot . . . for revolting indecent exposure of person to a little boy of tender years. It is a pity that someone had not been at hand to douse him with scalding water; and it would hardly have been inhuman to have set all the dogs of the town upon him if their instincts would have allowed them to bite his dirty carcass. He . . . was sentenced to one hundred days in the county jail. . . ."

Citation:

_____

Place:

_____

Topic:

_____

Subtopic:

_____

Quotation/Meaning:

_____

_____

24. *Placer County Republican,* June 10, 1885

"Michael Lemnell, who was shot some time ago by his son at Bath, and sent to the County Hospital, was discharged last week. While in the hospital he expressed great contrition for the conduct on his part which led to the shooting, but his repentance was only skin deep. He went home and thrashed his wife for which he has been committed to the County Jail for six months. He assumed the duties of his new position Saturday morning."

Citation:

_____

Place:

_____

Topic:

_____

Subtopic:

Name _____   **Instructor** _____   **Date**

Quotation/Meaning:

_____

_____

25. *Contra Costa County Gazette*, July 18, 1885

"John Bailey and William Sierp, two boys who burglarized T. Martin Woolbert's residence near Martinez a few weeks ago and were allowed to plead guilty of petit larceny and fined one dollar each on account of their youth, are now under $2,000 bonds in San Francisco for burglary. Two charges rest against Sierp. The boys are evidently young criminals of the worst order, and it is to be regretted that so much clemency was shown them here, now that their vicious propensities are so well known. At present they have a fair chance of obtaining an interior view of the large hotel at San Quentin."

Citation:

_____

Place:

_____

Topic:

_____

Subtopic:

_____

Quotation/Meaning:

_____

_____

26. *Julian Sentinel,* December 9, 1887

Dynamite: An Attempt is Made to Blow Up the American Bark Otage

"... there is a strong feeling of uneasiness among shipmasters in port, and this outrage added to the piratical proceedings on board the DARRA Saturday night will tend to give the port of San Diego a very bad name. ... The villainy enshrouded in the water front rabble in San Diego is rapidly becoming an unknown quantity, in fact it is the coming problem of '88 and when reduced to an uncommon fraction, will be found to contain Socialism, Nihilism and Anarchism combined with other disgusting isms which tend to create disturbances. This spirit of dictation-rule or ruin, the big I and the Little you, Have got to be set down, and the sooner the better. Down the triple headed monster at once and let the world know that San Diego boasts of a set of officers that is able and willing to protect her interests and the interest of the best harbor on the Pacific Coast."

Name   Instructor   Date

Citation:

_____

Place:

_____

Topic:

_____

Subtopic:

_____

Quotation/Meaning:

_____

_____

27. *Contra Costa County Gazette,* May 17, 1890
   "The acquittal of Geo. C. Pratt for the attempted killing of Bromwell, the Insurance President, is another evidence that there is an unwritten law regarded by the mass of mankind as above any statutory enactment. The man who invades the sanctity of another's home takes his life in his hand, and no sympathy is felt if swift retribution is visited upon him. As a sequel to this affair we notice that Pratt has filed an action for divorce. He professes to be solicitous for the future welfare of his wife, and is willing to give her a monthly allowance."

Citation:

_____

Place:

_____

Topic:

_____

Subtopic:

_____

Quotation/Meaning:

_____

_____

Name   **Instructor**   **Date**

28. *Julian Sentinel,* June 13, 1890

"Three specimens of man's greed and Indian's stupidity were locked up in the town jail last Sunday. On Monday they were brought into court and fined $12 each for drunkenness and indecent exposure which was paid for by their employers. Now, if those who furnished them the firewater could be caught and given the full extent of the law for such crime, we would have a little more quiet on our streets. It will be done sooner or later. . . . It is only a matter of time."

Citation:

_____

Place:

_____

Topic:

_____

Subtopic:

_____

Quotation/Meaning:

_____

_____

29. *Escondido Times,* June 16, 1892

"The rule of mob laws in this country seems to be extending. The fact that so many persons are lynched is the most powerful indictment that could be drawn up against the modes of criminal procedure prevalent everywhere. There cannot be any question of the fact that the machinery of the law, as it is administered in the United States, is cumbrous and slow, and provides more safeguards than terror for the criminal. A skillful criminal lawyer, if his client possesses any influence or standing whatever, can "wear out" any ordinary case, even murder. The law fills his hand with trump cards. He can find plenty of technicalities, a flaw in indictment, or some other legal quibble, and he can ask for new trials and appeals and postpone until important witnesses are dead or have left the country, and the public have forgotten the case."

Citation:

_____

Place:

_____

Topic:

_____

Subtopic:

_____

Quotation/Meaning:

_____

_____

30. *Contra Costa County Gazette,* July 5, 1890
    "The trial of Tom Young at Redding, for killing Sam Touton. . . . The jury acquitted him. Public sentiment has been with Young who killed Touton because of his making an indecent assault on his fourteen year-old daughter. Over sixty witnesses were examined. Upon the jury returning the verdict the large audience in the courtroom cheered lustily, and many hands were extended to Young and congratulations uttered."

Citation:

_____

Place:

_____

Topic:

_____

Subtopic:

_____

Quotation/Meaning:

_____

_____

31. *Escondido Times,* July 14, 1892
    "District Attorney General Johnstone Jones came up from San Diego Monday evening, at the request of Justice OGSBURY, for the purpose of prosecuting the criminal complaint sworn out by F.M. Jeffrey against J. Ruff for embezzlement . . . , set forth that J. RUFF had sold to G.W. COOK a cow on which JEFFREY had a bill of sale. On investigation the prosecuting attorney found that Mr. Ruff had not sold the cow, but had left it in possession of Mr. Cook, pending settlement of account and bill of sale held by Mr. Jeffrey. On Motion of Gen. Jones the case was dismissed. The county will have to foot the expense of witnesses, court and constable fees to the amount of sixty or seventy dollars. The county would be saved a great deal of

expense if the justices would investigate and use more discretion in issuing papers for criminal prosecutions."

Citation:

_____

Place:

_____

Topic:

_____

Subtopic:

_____

Quotation/Meaning:

_____

_____

32. *The Placer Argus,* March 3, 1893
Thin Out the Borders

"The following letter has been sent by District-Attorney Chamberlain to each Justice of the Peace in the county:
Office of the District Attorney of Placer County

Auburn, Cal., February 27, 1893

To the Justices of placer County:

MY DEAR JUDGE: My attention has been called to the large number of prisoners confined in the county jail during the months of January and February of this year; at one time reaching the large number of 41. Upon an examination of the commitments, I find the majority of the prisoners are committed for the offenses of vagrancy and fraudulently evading the payment of railroad fare, that he impose a sentence to the full extent of the law, and upon defendant promising forthwith to leave the county, he withhold the commitment a sufficient number of hours to permit the defendant to do so. This is intended to apply to the floating or tramp defendants, commonly known of as a "hobo." If you will give this procedure a trial, it is thereby hoped to save the transportation of the prisoners to the county jail and the board of the same while there.

Yours truly,

L. L. CHAMBERLAIN.

The object of this letter is, if possible to reduce the number of prisoners of the vagrant class in our county jail. The District Attorney says "when a defendant is found guilty of vagrancy or fraudulently evading the payment of railroad fare, sentence him to the full extent of the law, and upon his promise to leave the county, withhold the commitment a reasonable length of time that he may do so." In our opinion this would be the most effective way for the county; it would not only save the cost of transportation and mileage, but would also save the cost of boarding these "vags" for ten to thirty days at the rate of $3.00 per week.

We admit that a great many of those serving sentences as vagrants are the worst criminal class, many whom are wanted elsewhere for crimes committed, but the majority are of that order who are constantly after but never overtake a job.

There is no reason why the taxpayers should year after year furnish a lodging house and restaurant for this class of people. . . ."

Citation:

_____

Place:

_____

Topic:

_____

Subtopic:

_____

Quotation/Meaning:

_____

33. *Contra Costa County Gazette*, May 4, 1895

"Two brutal murderers, condemned to be hung on Friday, have been respited for a month by the Governor. Their lives have already been prolonged upon one pretense or another, and it now looks as if their chances for reasonable longevity is about as good as that of average men."

Citation:

_____

Place:

_____

Topic:

_____

Subtopic:

_____

Quotation/Meaning:

_____

34. *Contra Costa County Gazette,* December 31, 1898

This Year's Record of Lynching

"So far as the records have been completed 121 malefactors or supposed male-factors were executed without process of law during the present year. Possibly several innocent persons were executed by mobs of well meaning men who were blinded by passion, but the truth will never be known. Lynching is in general a bad habit. The fact that it is prevalent in particular localities does not indicate that crime is rampant in those places; neither does it indicate that the people who participate in lawless executions are altogether depraved or dangerous. When a particularly atrocious crime is committed in any locality, there are always hot-headed individuals who shout for summary vengeance. If the offender is locked up in a strong jail in charge of a resolute sheriff, the men who clamor for lynch-law usually come to their senses before harm is done. If the jail is a rickety structure which may easily be penetrated by a mob, there is often a lynching bee.

In seventy-five per cent of the cases in the south and west mob violence is invited by poor jails. In frontier towns the people are impatient at the delays of the law, and the fear that the criminal will escape through departure of necessary witnesses or through some technicality leads to lynching. . . ."

Citation:

_____

Place:

_____

Topic:

_____

Subtopic:

_____

Quotation/Meaning:

_____

_____

35. *Santa Ana Bulletin,* December 28, 1899

Sympathy or Slush

(The case of Katie Cook of "Peatlands" for killing her husband while he slept.)

". . .The case has naturally created a great sensation. Public opinion often justi-fies the man who slaps the wretch that has broken up and ruined his home; but what will it say of the woman who killed a husband flagrantly and brazenly faith-less to her and flaunted his sin almost before her eyes? But then there is the law. . . . . Katie Cook's testimony of "marital infidelity and the cruelty and threats of her husband, coupled with his bestiality did much to bring about a speedy verdict. One of the jurymen said he way sorry the jury could not vote Mrs. Cook a medal for killing her husband."

Citation:

_____

Place:

_____

Topic:

_____

Subtopic:

_____

Quotation/Meaning:

_____

_____

Exercise 2

Make a list of the topics and subtopics that you have identified in each of the thirty-five documents above. Then list those topics from broadest to narrowest, do the same with the subtopics. Now think of several categories and determine how many of your topics and subtopics fit under each of those. As you work your lists will begin to form a visual matrix that looks something like this:

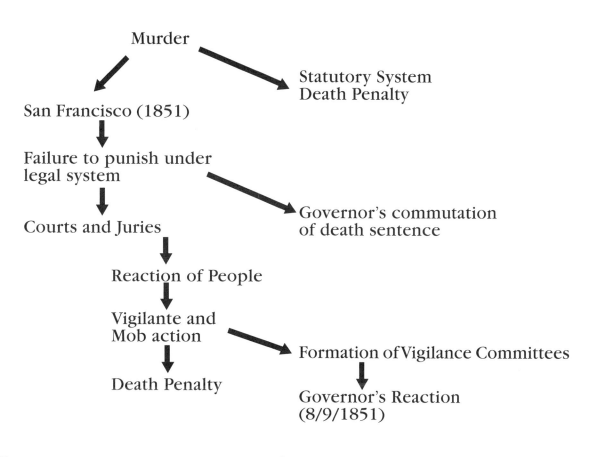

Name   **Instructor**   **Date**

For example, you may wish to identify crime as one of your principal categories and criminal justice as a subcategory of it: do any of the topics or subtopics you have already listed fit under one or the other or both? Can you think of any subcategories of the subcategory? How many of your topics and subtopics fit under this one? Extend this exercise as far as you can, attaching separate sheets of paper as needed. We will help you get started, but you should do your best to complete our lists before trying a pyramid of your own.

Category 1: CRIME
Complete the list of the crimes mentioned in the texts of documents.

1. Murder

2. Assault

3. Robbery

4.

5.

6.

7.

8.

9.

10.

Now organize these crimes under the following subcategories. (Do your best to complete the lists; you will find that some of the crimes fit under two or more different categories.)

Subcategory 1: CRIMES AGAINST PERSONS. Complete the list.

1. Rape [Sexual Assault]

2.

3.

4.

5.

Subcategory 2: CRIMES AGAINST PROPERTY. Complete the list.

1. Theft

2.

3.

4.

5.

Subcategory 3: CRIMES AGAINST MORALITY, PUBLIC ORDER, OR LEGAL ORDER. Complete the list.

1. Gambling

2.

3.

4.

5.

    Now go back to your original lists, or the documents themselves, and consider narrower categories. Be certain to read the documents carefully to accurately determine exactly who and what is represented in the newspaper stories.

List the persons accused of crime.

1. Immigrants from the penal colonies

2. Waterfront rabble

3.

4.

5.

6.

7.

8.

List the victims of crime.

1. Mrs. Margarita Temple, wife of Francisco Temple

2. William Carey Jones

3.

4.

5.

Copyright © 1999 Harlan Davidson, Inc.

Name   Instructor   Date

6.

7.

8.

9.

List the editorial comments on popular justice.

1. Hanging of McCauley (why?)

2. "Lynching [is] a bad habit."

3.

4.

5.

List the institutions of law cited.

1. Courts . . . problems and promise of

2. The Governor . . . (What is his problem?)

3.

4.

5.

List the penalties those convicted faced.

1. Death . . . for which crimes, when?

2.

3.

4.

List examples of disparate justice, a denial of equal protection under the law and/ or due process of law.

1. Chinese gamblers

2. Pancho Daniel's "trial"

3.

4.

Name   Instructor   Date

5.

6.

Now ask yourself what relationships exist between and among the historical facts listed above. Can you restructure the lists to create a meaningful picture/ matrix of the criminal justice system? You may need to use separate sheets of paper to complete this exercise. Remember how crime statistics displayed in Chapter Six created questions about representations and meanings. Be certain to consider these problems in your criminal justice portrait.

Name   Instructor   Date

Exercise 3

Do some reading in the secondary literature on one or more of the topics you have identified to determine how our attitudes about crime have changed in the last one hundred years. Write a research report on your findings.

Your report should be seven to twelve pages long and include reference to at least one of the titles listed below, as well as your own interpretation of the documents in this chapter.

Be certain to establish a formal bibliography (like in the form of the list below) of the sources you consulted.

You may wish to consult one or more of the following:

Ethington, Philip J., "Vigilantes and the Police: The Creation of a Professional Police Bureaucracy in San Francisco, 1847–1900," *Journal of Social History* 21 (Winter, 1987), pp. 197-227.

Hartog, Hendrik, "Lawyering, Husbands' Rights, and "the Unwritten Law" in Nineteenth-Century America," *The Journal of American History* 84 (June, 1997), pp. 67–96.

Johnson, David A., "Vigilance and the Law: The Moral Authority of Popular Justice in the Far West," *American Quarterly* 33 (Winter, 1981), pp. 558–85.

McGrath, Roger D., *Gunfighters, Highwaymen & Vigilantes: Violence on the Frontier* (Berkeley: University of California Press, 1984).

Mullen, Kevin J., *Let Justice Be Done: Crime and Politics in Early San Francisco* (Reno: University of Nevada Press, 1989).

Senkewicz, Robert M., S. J., *Vigilantes in Gold Rush San Francisco* (Stanford: Stanford University Press, 1985).

Writing California History: Your Turn

Good history starts with good writing. This book forces you to think critically in the process of doing historical research. Chapter Three suggested some research topics, and subsequent chapters may have sparked an interest in others. Regardless of the topic you chose to investigate or the nature of the project assigned to you in this course, you must express the end product of your research in writing. What, you may well ask, do instructors expect of my writing? How will my paper or essay be graded? The following rubric for assessing student work is drawn from one developed by Angela Henderson at Mount San Antonio College, Walnut, California.

What Instructors Expect

The "A" paper (or essay): This work is well written, thoughtfully organized, and clearly demonstrates strong critical-thinking skills. The essay has a clear thesis statement (a clearly stated interpretation of the topic of the paper) contained in the first paragraph of the paper (the introduction). All of the paragraphs that follow (the body of the paper) are composed in support of the thesis. Each paragraph is not unlike a tiny essay, for each has a topic sentence, a body of evidence in support of the topic sentence, and a conclusory sentence or transition that links it to the following paragraph. Throughout, the writing maintains a particular style, manner, or tone appropriate to the subject matter and keeps the interest of the reader. Transitional words and phrases smoothly move the reader through the paper. Finally, the last paragraph of the work (the conclusion) efficiently summarizes the thesis, restates key points of evidence, and relates the author's own interpretation of the evidence displayed. The "A" paper contains few, if any, errors in grammar, spelling, or punctuation.

The "B" paper: This work is not truly a complete one because it fails to support adequately (the evidence is questionable or poorly presented) all or most of the aspects of its stated thesis. This paper is not very well organized; mechanical and grammatical errors are extant but do not interfere with the author's organization or content.

The "C" paper: This paper also needs more work, and the thesis itself is unclear and almost all of the paragraphs are inadequately structured to support it. Evidence is not detailed, and historic facts are not established; transitions are weak or fail to exist, and errors in the conventions of written English are numerous enough to distract the reader greatly.

The "D" and "F" papers and beyond ("G," "H," "I," "J," "K"—Professor Bakken employs a ten-part letter scale, awarding numeric grades below "F" to deserving students): These papers contain only one or two of the "A"-paper criteria and in varying degrees fail to demonstrate even a basic understanding of the conventions of written English.

A Word on Style

Instructors expect sentences to be clear, varied, and grammatically correct. Practice word economy: make your point in as few words as possible. Vary the structure of your sentences and, when possible, avoid using the same word or phrase repeatedly or in close proximity. Further, to keep the reader's attention, try to write in positive terms and use the active voice. For example, compare the following versions of the same sentence. Which one packs more punch?

Jordan's performance tonight was not a disappointment to the fans who were thrilled to see it.

Jordan thrilled the fans tonight.

Unless you like having your time wasted, you probably prefer the second, active version. Note that even though the second sentence is much shorter than the first, it conveys every bit as much information.

When proofreading your first draft, look for forms of the verb "Be" (is, was, were, had been, would have been) in your sentences. These words may indicate use of the passive voice. Here's another example:

The active voice was not used by the student.

The student used the passive voice.

Again, the second version is positive, active, and easier to read and understand. Also, it is generally good style to keep the acting agent of the sentence at its beginning, as its subject. Obviously, the passive voice has many legitimate uses (as this sentence attests) and it is not imperative that it be entirely avoided. Nonetheless, stay attuned to the matter and choose the active voice whenever possible. Once you get into this habit—one that admittedly takes a good deal of practice—your writing will improve greatly.

Instructors expect you to use good grammar. Some of the most common errors we see in student papers and essays are tense shifts, fragmented sentences, agreement problems (subject and verb do not agree because the subject is, for example, singular and the verb is plural), punctuation errors (especially misuse of the semicolon before transitional connectives), misuse of the possessive pronoun (its, which is a possessive pronoun confused with it's, a contraction of it is), run-on sentences, comma splice errors, dangling participles (when a participle phrase beginning a sentence does not refer to the subject—for example, "Short of breath and full of oats, the man decided to let the horse rest for a while."), misused articles, ambiguous and improper case of pronouns, and preposition errors. Hopefully, most of this sounds familiar, echoing back from a past English class.

If you think you could use a bit more help in the basic mechanics of writing English—and *everyone* could—take an hour or so to read *The Elements of Style* by William Strunk Jr. and E. B. White. This remarkable little book offers simple, practical advice on all of "the rules of usage and principles of composition most commonly violated."[1] In addition to offering clear, practical advice on how to write well, "Strunk & White" is great fun to read.

---

1. William Strunk Jr. and E. B. White, *The Elements of Style,* 3d ed. (Needham Heights, Mass.: Allyn and Bacon, 1995).

The Writing Process

After days or weeks of research it's time to write. First, organize your research notes. In the process of taking notes on each source you found, you gave each note card a topic heading followed by subtopics and listed at least three key words in your description. Your note cards on secondary sources bear citations in bibliographic form: author, title, place of publication, publisher, date of publication. You also have identified a citation, place, topic, and at least one subtopic for each primary source you interrogated. If you took your notes on a computer, you can sort them in any number of ways, but you still should print out a hard copy for use back in the field (be it library, historical society, or other). If you used paper note cards, you may have to resort them many times during the planning of your paper, unless you created note cards with single-topic headings. For example, Professor Bakken wrote the *California Legal History Manuscripts in the Huntington Library: A Guide* (San Marino: The Huntington Library Press, 1989). In that book he created subject headings for each document and recorded the collection name, box number, and date. A finder's aid further described the subject matter of the document. To give a concrete example of such an entry, on page 156 of that book you will find the topic (real property) followed by the title (regarding the transfer of a deed to Ranch Jesus Maria by the firm of Halleck, Peachy and Billings, 1839–1841). The entry looks like this:

Subject Hdgs./ Subdivision	Collection	Box	Date	Finder's Aid
REAL PROPERTY *(Topic)*				
Title *(Subtopic)*	Halleck, Peachy, Billings	1	1839–41	Transfer Deed to Rancho Jesus Maria; various documents

Halleck . . . that name may spark a memory of a man looking for a wife in 1849 and supporting Married Women's Property law to draw women west [chapter 3].[2]

After your note cards are spread out on a table or printed out in topical and subtopical order, organize, and then reorganize, those notes. The process of reading the cards and sorting them into an organizational matrix of your own design will refresh your memory of things read and keyboarded weeks ago. The process also sharpens your critical-thinking skills, forcing you to make hundreds of keen decisions regarding the piles of information you gathered. If your table or desktop is too small to accommodate all of your notes, spread them out on the floor and get down there with them. Now visualize their relationships. Start arranging the note cards in sequential stacks based on relationships of topic or time. For example, if you are writing a paper on the history of the struggle for women's rights in California, your research started with sources relating our Hispanic heritage.[3] You also took notes on the 1849 Constitutional Convention and the 1878–79 convention. The politicization of women in San Francisco in the 1880s probably gen-

2. Halleck would later become President Lincoln's chief of staff and earn the nickname "Old Brains." James M. McPherson, *Battle Cry of Freedom: The Civil War Era* (New York: Oxford University Press, 1988), pp. 331, 394, 488, 502, 524, 718. To the point of the history of the 1849 provision, you did find Donna C. Schuele, "Community Property Law and the Politics of Married Women's Rights in Nineteenth-Century California," *Western Legal History* 7 (1994), 245.
3. Perhaps you consulted David Langum, *Law and Community in Mexican California* (Norman: University of Oklahoma Press, 1989).

erated a substantial number of notes.[4] Further, the 1896 campaign for woman suffrage, an important historical watershed deserving analysis, spawned more notes.[5] Then the 1849 prediction of a need for a liberal divorce law came true, adding to the number of sources you had to consult and assess.[6] As the number of topical piles grows, you further divide them into subtopics and find synchronic (chronological) relationships. Public policy formation flowed from numerous streams of interest and found confluence in statutes and constitutional amendments. Now your arrangement of note cards starts to resemble a great tree with branches aloft, or a great river with tributaries flowing down into an ever-expanding torrent of meaning. As you get down to the base of the tree, or the mouth of the river . . . you find a thesis! Traveling back up the trunk and into the branches, the piles of notes in topical/date order offer an outline of paragraphs, which, through your interpretation, lead to a conclusion. In other words, the process of sorting note cards on the table or in a computer program slowly moves you to generalization as well as to specific topics and themes. The broadest generalization may bring you to a thesis statement, which, as mentioned, you will present in your introductory paragraph.

A good introductory paragraph begins with a good topic sentence, as is the case with all of the paragraphs that follow it. With all of your note cards in your hand or spread out on the table or monitor, you need to summarize their content and meaning. The generalization about those few pieces of historical evidence should constitute part of your thesis, the meaning of the pieces forms the other part. That meaning courses from the good historical questions you asked in the process of research and flows into your thesis and into each topic sentence in your paper or essay. Sentences, expository in nature, form the body of each paragraph and link the evidence to the topic sentence, which asserts your interpretation of the evidence in historical context. Sometimes the evidence establishing a historical fact might stem from so many different sources that citing one or two representative source quotations is more appropriate than listing evidentiary quotations from each source. Obviously, each source of additional evidence should be cited in a footnote. For example, looking back on the note card exercise in Chapter Seven, you could use fifteen evidentiary quotations from the fifteen primary-source documents reproduced there to make a point about crime, but that would make your paper needlessly long and discursive. Instead, find one quotation that closely supports your thesis, use it, and cite other similar documents in a footnote.

When incorporating quotations into the body of your paper, introduce each one with a signal phrase telling the reader how it relates to the topic of the paragraph or helps establish the context of your subject. Then insert the quotation. A rule of thumb is that quotations of three lines or less should be kept within the body of the paragraph, enclosed in quotation marks, and followed directly by a footnote number, at the end of the quotation. If the quotation is more than three lines long, you should present it as a block quote, indented and single-spaced without quotation marks. Block quotes are preceded by a colon and they, too, must conclude with a footnote number. A block quote looks like the following (opposite):

4. Philip J. Ethington, *The Public City: The political construction of urban life in San Francisco, 1850–1900* (New York: Cambridge University Press, 1994), pp. 326-36.
5. Susan Scheiber Edelman, "'A Red Hot Suffrage Campaign': The Woman Suffrage Cause in California, 1896," *The California Supreme Court Historical Society Yearbook 1995* 2, pp. 51-131.
6. Glenda Riley, *Divorce: An American Tradition* (New York: Oxford University Press, 1991), pp. 90-5, 120, 156, 163-6.

> The next sentence following the block quote, which should not begin
> a new paragraph, should explain the language of the quotation and its
> relevance to the topic sentence. Regardless of the form they take, quota
> tions should not be allowed to stand alone.[fn]

You are the historian and you have the obligation of telling the reader how the quotation fits and what it means, even if the statement is absolutely clear to you.

Remember that the paragraph is a rhetorical building block seeking to establish the authority of your interpretation. You are building a case for a very sophisticated jury or a single expert judge. You need to tell the reader exactly what evidence you have for the interpretation asserted in your thesis.

What if in the course of your research you have found evidence contrary to the interpretation for which you are building a case? Do you simply look the other way and intentionally fail to mention the existence of that evidence in your paper? No. Acting as a historian, you must account for that evidence in an ethical, professional manner. Remember, causation is seldom singular, and historians, as social scientists, have acknowledged that human events are complex. Therefore, present any contrary evidence but refute it as best you can. In the process, you should explain why the logic presented by some sources is flawed or faulty. Explain the contrary evidence in expository sentences. Compare it to the other evidence you have uncovered. Tell your reader clearly why you believe your interpretation better represents causation. We want you to explain your argument. Argument is, after all, central to a sound historical thesis.

Now that you have written all of these paragraphs about topics and themes, it is time to review your work and your thinking on the evidence. This will form the content of your conclusion. Here you are not a lawyer arguing for all of the evidence supporting your client's position; you are a scholar presenting your interpretation of why events took place and what that meant, or means, to society. You have all of the evidence and you are trying to explain why women failed to gain the vote in the 1896 California election, yet succeeded during the Progressive era. You have found linkages to the temperance movement commingled with women's rights issues and you have numerous references to birth control, abortion, employment, education, child care, and public health issues. How do all these subtopics fit together and why were women successful at one time and not at another if all of their demands were so right, so powerful, so destined for success? As you wrote paragraphs on each issue, breaking each one down into topics, subtopics, and themes, your appreciation of the complexity of the political process deepened.

Frankly, historians frequently start from two very different points in research, and you should not feel overwhelmed by the complexity of the issues you may uncover. Some scholars wish to disprove the thesis of another historian or of an ideological school of historical thought. They search for all of the evidence extant in constructing a predetermined thesis. Others become fascinated with a topic of interest and embark on decades of research and writing in search of its historical meaning. The now-famous historian Frederick Jackson Turner announced in 1893 that the very existence of a "frontier" formed American democracy and molded the American character. One hundred years later, historians of the American West still debate Turner's thesis. Some start with the thesis that Turner was wrong and proceed from there. Others research a particular topic in western history for many years; only after extensive inquiry do they presume to make judgments on Turner's thesis. California history is similarly filled with good historical theses worth consideration.

Exercises

Exercise 1

Read the following excerpted documents and, on separate sheets of paper, write five paragraphs on their content and possible meaning. Be certain to address specific topics raised by the sources such as the death penalty, civil liability, and gender. Although the sources below are quite different, they are contemporaneous and provide a good starting point if you wish to understand present-day California politics.

1. Pat Soberanis, "A California Journal Survey: How biased is the Court?," *California Journal* (September, 1986), pp. 435-7.

"Most of the campaign against Supreme Court Chief Justice Rose Bird has focused on her decisions in criminal cases. Her opponents claim Bird has gone out of her way to protect the rights of criminals, even if that means hampering prosecutors. Public opinion polls reflect this view; an August California Poll showed that 62 percent of voters feel Bird has "gone too far in protecting criminal defendants." p. 435

"...85 percent of Chief Justice Bird's decisions tend to favor prosecutors, and that her decision-making, as a whole, is not much different than that of other justices. It is also significant to note that her written opinions overwhelmingly favor defendants and that, in this area, she differs greatly from some of her colleagues." p. 437

2. Barry Winograd, "Bird, Grodin, Reynoso: Are they a 'gang of three'?," *California Journal* (September, 1986), pp. 439-41.

"The statistical evidence does not support the claim that Jerry Brown bequeathed a set of judicial clones who share views dramatically isolated from others on the Court. This, being so, it places an added burden on the justices' opponents to explain why all three justices should be attacked as a group. The November reconfirmation election results may well depend on opponents' ability to make that case or to obscure the differences so the public does not notice." p. 441

3. A. G. Block, "A status report on the death penalty in California," *California Journal* (September, 1986), pp. 443-5.

"The campaign to oust Bird and two of her colleagues (Joseph Grodin and Cruz Reynoso) has crystallized around the death penalty. Their foes hammer at the Court's record, arguing that California lags far behind other states in executing criminals because of the Court's anti-death-penalty bias." p. 443

4. Rivian Taylor and James Richardson, "Rose Bird and the Media: Stalking the wily chief justice," *California Journal* (September, 1986), pp. 451-5.

"Still, the hallmark of her press relations has been a certain awkwardness. Often she has not answered an interviewer's questions so much as used them as a springboard for long winded dissertations on the institution of the Court and inadequacies of the electoral process for judges. She has complained that coverage of her and the Court has been superficial; that, for instance, the media has concentrated on her new flashy hair style. News coverage, she said in an October 1985 speech, is 'a barrage of intrusive trivialities . . . substituted for any discussion of ideas about matters of public concern.'" p. 452

5. Bob Egelko, "Standing in Dispute: The Court's national stature has waned under Bird," *California Journal* (September, 1986), pp. 428-33.

"The Bird Court is known as a civil plaintiff's Court—but some of its most significant civil-law rulings of the 1980s upheld state laws restricting the right to sue doctors and hospitals for malpractice." p. 428

6. Richard Zeiger, "Judgement Day for the Supreme Court: Rose Bird faces the ultimate jury," *California Journal* (September, 1986), pp. 423-7.

"Barring a remarkable political turnaround, the state's voters this November will—for the first time—refuse a new term to an unopposed appellate court justice. In the view of some, that's an event which will permanently alter the state's judiciary, upsetting the delicate balance between the branches of government and leaving every judge to ponder if his or her next decision will unleash the voter's wrath." p. 423

7. Richard Zeiger, "Duke's Landslide: Second term blessed by complacent electorate," *California Journal* (December, 1986), pp. 579-81.

"For Deukmejian, the biggest change in the next four years may not be in his own branch of government, but in the judiciary where he has the opportunity to reshape the state's Supreme Court in his own image. The appointment of a new chief justice will come soon, with speculation centering on the two justices he has already appointed, Malcolm Lucas and Edward Panelli. Choices for the three remaining justices will come later."

8. Susan Yoachum, "Duke's Court veers to right," *California Journal* (June, 1987), pp. 299-300.

"The most obvious difference between the Lucas Court and the Bird Court is that the court is now without a female member for the first time since Bird was appointed in 1977. Although Deukmejian ignored the pressure to name a woman to the state's highest court, he did retain Hispanic representation on the court with the appointment of Arguelles." p. 300

9. Robert Egelko, "The Duke puts a new face on the Supreme Court," *California Journal* (June, 1988), pp. 236-40.

"The Court moved decisively if not uniformly to the right; it has upheld most but not all death sentences, and established an air of harmony among its members and the legal community.

The controversy that seemed to attend every action of the Bird Court has disappeared. Rulings by the Lucas Court occasionally draw criticism but don't seem to stir public anger." p. 236

10. Gerald F. Uelmen, "Mainstream Justice: A review of the second year of the Lucas Court," *California Lawyer* (June, 1989), pp. 37-41.

"The Lucas Court is affirming the underlying first-degree murder conviction at a rate of 95 percent. It has not reversed a single finding of special circumstances under the Briggs initiative. Thus, most reversals have simply been on the penalty phase, and required a remand only for a new penalty trial. The affirmance rate of 76 percent on penalty phase issues, compared to the 17 percent rate of the Bird Court, is unquestionably due to a different perspective of the standard for harmless error."

11. Robert Egelko, "The Supreme Court's revolving door: Is all the turnover good for the high Court?," *California Journal* (July 1990), pp. 347–52.

"The departures [of Justices Arguelles, Kaufman, and Eagleson] . . . were a sign that the death penalty, the downfall of the Bird Court, continues to serve up an intractable problem for the state's judiciary." pp. 347–8

12. Robert Egelko, "A low-profile court: Since Rose Bird's departure, the California Supreme Court has been less controversial, and less visible," *California Journal* (June, 1994), pp. 35–8.

"Largely by upholding death sentences, the court headed by Chief Justice Malcolm Lucas for the last several years has managed to avoid the prominence and controversy that surrounded the Rose Bird court in the years leading up to the 1986 elections, when Bird and two colleagues were voted out of office. A return to a lower profile was probably healthy for the court and certainly welcomed by the justices. But the Lucas court is an important force in the state, and it's hard to understand its near-invisibility." p. 35

Stanley Mosk was part of the Culbert Olson administration in the 1930s, was attorney general of California when "Pat" Brown was elected governor, and played a major role in the Bird Court investigation.

13. Steve Scott, "Battle of the Black Hats: Tort reform dogfight could escalate into all-out initiative war," *California Journal* (June, 1995), pp. 8-12.

"What is wrong with the legal liability system? Well, according to businesses and insurance companies, it boils down to too many lawsuits with not enough merit seeking too much in damages."

Exercise 2

Research the following in the library or online and answer the following: Did the Lucas Court substantially change the precedents of the Bird Court in civil liability cases?

Los Angeles Times, November 2, 1986, Part 8, page 5
The San Diego Union-Tribune, August 19, 1988, page A-3
Los Angeles Times, Jan 1, 1989, Part 1, page 3
Los Angeles Times, February 6, 1991, Part D, page 3
Los Angeles Times, January 12, 1989, Part 2, page 6
Los Angeles Times, September 8, 1993, Part A, page 1
The Recorder, December 17, 1993, page 1
The Recorder, Dec. 30, 1993, page 1
The Fresno Bee, January 3, 1994, page 4
The Recorder, June 1, 1994, page 1
The Recorder, October 28, 1994, page 1
Los Angeles Times, August 22, 1995, Part A, page 1

The Recorder, September 1, 1995, page 1
The San Diego Union-Tribune, September 3, 1995, page H-3

TO GO DEEPER:
Read the following for a greater understanding of the politics of judicial elections:
Betty Medsger, *Framed: The New Right Attack on Chief Justice Rose Bird and the Courts* (New York: Pilgrim Press, 1983).
Preble Stoltz, *Judging Judges* (New York: Free Press, 1981).
Brenda Farrington, "Credibility and Crisis in California's High Court," in John W. Johnson, ed., *Historic U.S. Court Cases, 1690–1990: An Encyclopedia* (New York: Garland Publishing, 1992), pp. 51–4.

Optional Exercise

Read the following for a multidisciplinary understanding of the death penalty in history and politics:
Michel Foucault, *Discipline and Punish: The Birth of the Prison* (New York: Vintage Books, 1979). This will provide the Postmodern view.
William J. Bowers, "Capital Punishment and Contemporary Values: People's Misgivings and the Courts Mispreceptions," *Law and Society Review* 27 (1993), pp. 157–75.
Phoebe C. Ellsworth and Samuel R. Gross, "Hardening of Attitudes: Americans' Views on the Death Penalty," *Journal of Social Issues* 50 (1994), pp. 19–45.
Edmund F. McGarrell and Maria Sandys, "The Misperception of Public Opinion Toward the Death Penalty," *American Behavioral Scientist* 39 (1996), pp. 500–13.

Exercise 3

Write a paper on the public image of Rose Bird, 1977–97, using newspapers, periodicals, law reviews, and other print media paying particular attention to issues of gender.

Compare Bird's developed image in the print media with the image of other women serving on the California Supreme Court.

Exercise 4

In order to answer the questions that follow, research the 1950 United States Senate campaign between Richard M. Nixon and Helen Gahagan Douglas. Be certain to consult the *People's Daily World* as well as the mainstream newspapers of California. In addition, read *Newsweek,* August 28, 1950, page 84. For reflective commentary on the election and its meaning, see Helen Gahagan Douglas, *A Full Life* (Garden City, N.Y.: Doubleday & Co., 1983) and Richard Nixon, *Richard Nixon: The Memoirs of Richard Nixon* (New York: Simon & Schuster, 1990 Richard Nixon Library Edition). Also see Ingrid W. Scobie, *Center Stage: Helen Gahagan Douglas, A Life* (New York: Oxford University Press, 1992).

What were the issues in the campaign?

_____

_____

What public image did each candidate endeavor to create? What image did each attempt to cast on the other?

_____

Name _____ **Instructor** _____ **Date**

How did international events influence the election?

_____

_____

Was gender a factor in this election?

_____

Why?

_____

_____

Representative
Loretta Sanchez.
Courtesy Office of
Congresswoman
Loretta Sanchez.

Exercise 5

In order to answer the questions that follow, research the Robert Dornan-Loretta Sanchez Congressional election of 1996 in the press and periodical literature.

Newsweek, November 25, 1996, quoted Dornan as saying in 1994 that "every lesbian spear-chucker in the country is hoping I get defeated." Was Representative Dornan basing this observation on evidence you can find in a literature search about opposition to him?

_____

_____

_____

_____

Cite your sources.

_____

_____

_____

What demographic factors enabled Sanchez's victory at the polls?

_____

Cite your sources.

_____

_____

_____

What did Representative Dornan do after the defeat at the polls?
Note: Be certain to consult the Federal Document Clearing House as a source of information on this issue.

_____

_____

_____

What did the House Oversight Committee Task Force for the Contested Election in the 46th Congressional District do regarding this election?

_____

_____

Cite your sources:

_____

_____

_____

TO GO DEEPER:
See Vicki L. Ruiz, *From Out of the Shadows: Mexican Women in Twentieth Century America* (New York: Oxford University Press, 1998), pp. 124–46, regarding Mexican-American women "claiming public space."

Optional Exercise

Exercise 6
Read the following and look for the issues that made Progressivism distinct in California politics.

1. *San Francisco Chronicle,* November 1, 1910: Republican Leader Brands the Railroad Stock Story as "Perfidious Lie"

"It is a perfidious lie from beginning to end," said Johnson regarding Frank Herring's speech that he was paid $55,000 in Western Pacific stock for defending Dalzell Brown. "I never received such a fee, and neither do I own stock in the Western Pacific." He said "the whole story was manufactured by my political enemies, who are doing everything they can to injure me. My most bitter enemies in the State are such men as [Abraham] Ruef and [William] Herrin. Their attacks will do them no good, as the best people in the State are with me in this fight."

Name _____   **Instructor** _____   **Date** _____

2. *San Francisco Chronicle,* November 3, 1910: The Republican Candidate Says That the State Outside San Francisco Has Already Made Its Choice

"The contest has been transmuted now in San Francisco into a struggle between the special interests, and every representative of the special interests, and every man, and newspaper that thrives by wrongdoing and crookedness, on the one hand, and myself on the other."

3. *San Francisco Chronicle,* November 4, 1910: Hiram Johnson Answers Questions of His Opponent

"Today special interest is at bay in California. It is the last ditch; making its death struggle, just as it has been in Washington, in Colorado, Wisconsin and in Kansas, and where the pioneer of the people's rights is leading the battle. Today in New York the same fight is on, where that titanic figure of the world's history is making our fight. I hope we shall see the same triumph in New York which we are to witness in California next Tuesday.

Today the beast is at bay here in San Francisco, and as ever he had turned polecat, and is belching forth billingsgate in the effort to elect that man Governor who is going to put out [of] the State of California this same beast.

You need not fear that which they may do in San Francisco. Whatever Abraham Ruef and Patrick Calhoun and William Randolph Hearst may do in San Francisco they cannot yet elect a Governor of California. . . ."

"These people hope to divert you and all the people of this State. The problem that is for you to solve is that which we solved so well as the primary—of driving out William F. Herrin and the Southern Pacific from the government of the State, and we have driven them from the Republican party."

4. *San Francisco Chronicle,* November 6, 1910 Political Advertisement, page 55

"Never in a modern republic was democracy, the freedom of the people to govern themselves, so bitterly and so desperately assailed by deadly conspiracy between the tories of politics, corrupt financiers and the mob of the tenderloin.

This amazing spectacle, this stupendous intrigue, is flaunted in your faces.

The deaf and the blind need not be deceived. All the power of corporate wealth represented by the greatest transcontinental railroad in the country, represented further by the syndicated capital that monopolizes the street railway franchises of a dozen great cities; represented further by Hearst, the Democrat, has time and again repudiated his party, the better to gratify his passion to rule or ruin; represented further by Abraham Ruef, that convicted and unjailed political boss and felon who brazenly walks the streets of San Francisco, out on bail, working with all his old-time craft and cunning to rally his henchmen in the great struggle of the political indecencies against law and order; represented further by all the "bawds" of journalism and all the spawn of the political underworld are banded together.

There you have the line-up.

And who is the storm center of all this onslaught?

Against Hiram W. Johnson is arrayed all this mendacity, all these franchise thieves, all these predatory financiers, all these political corruptionists; all these assassins of character, all these unjailed felons that have shamed San Francisco before the whole world.

No higher tribute was ever paid to any man in the State of California than today, the promiscuous infamies of San Francisco are paying to Hiram W. Johnson in their clamorous opposition to him."

5. *Sacramento Bee,* September 22, 1914
Republicans Villify Johnson for Freak Legislation
and Then Claim All Credit For It

"Governor Hiram W. Johnson resumed his campaign for re-election, here [Lodi] tonight in a stirring speech in which he set forth that his two opponents of the Democratic and Republican parties were combined in a fight against him on the principles of the old bi-partisan machine that either one of the two reactionaries may win but a reformer never. . . .

Johnson said, "Are you aware that this platform of Milton Schmitt and Eddie Wolfe claims that all that was done in the past four years was done by them? Now if all that was done during the past four years was done by them and well done, in the name of Heaven can you explain to me why it was that for doing those things we were abused and vilified.""

6. *Sacramento Bee,* October 2, 1914
Legislation Favoring Wage Earners Passed in Johnson's Term

"The following are some of the measures passed during the administration of Governor Hiram Johnson and endorsed by Organized Labor:

Raising the rates of taxation on public-service corporations for the support of the State.

Blue Sky Law: To protect investors in corporate securities and to prevent fraud.

Establishing a Legislative Counsel Bureau to assist in the drafting of proper legislation.

Appointment and organization of a new State Board of Education.

Empowering the Railroad Commission to value public utilities to be condemned by counties or municipalities.

Strengthening the Tenement House Act, creating better sanitary housing conditions.

Selection of School Text Books to give preference to California authors.

Establishment of a Department of Tuberculosis under control of the State Board of Health.

Prohibiting the exportation of abalones, an anti-alien proposition.

Abolishing the straitjackets and other cruel punishments in the State Prisons.

Providing for a Water Commission to conserve the water power of the State.

Establishing a Board of Parole Commissioners and prescribing rules to govern.

Establishing State inspection of weights and measures, benefiting all consumers.

Establishing a teachers' pension. Endorsed by the San Francisco Labor Council."

7. *San Francisco Chronicle,* October 4, 1914
Fredericks Finds Triumph Waiting in Capital

"Captain [John D.] Fredericks was elated today when he received a stenographic report of the speech delivered by Johnson at Riverside and a perusal of it showed that it was nothing but a lot of bombastic verbiage that had nothing to do with the issues of the campaign.

Incidentally, Johnson had ceased proclaiming that he is entitled to credit for all the good laws on the states books of the State, Fredericks' exposition of the facts having proved effective."

8. *San Francisco Chronicle,* October 8, 1914
What Johnson Costs California

"It is not surprising that Hiram Johnson goes up and down the State denouncing all whom he does not control. It is the regular criminal lawyer habit—if you

Copyright © 1999 Harlan Davidson, Inc.

have no case, abuse the other fellow. Bluster and ribald abuse of opponents is the Johnson method of diverting attention from his own extravagance. . . .

We challenge Hiram Johnson to produce the details of his personal traveling and other expenses since he has been Governor and which the people have paid that it may be known how much of what the people paid was expended for business of the State and how much for the promotion of the Johnson brand of politics."

9. *San Francisco Chronicle,* October 19, 1914

THE POLITICAL MACHINE OF HIRAM JOHNSON. It Is the Most Tremendous, Unscrupulous and Devastating State Machine on Earth.

". . . in three and a half years his administration has raised the State payroll by $2,336,193 and the number of State employees from 4230 to nearly 6000. . . .

In the unparalleled turpitude of Governor Johnson in applying to his own private purposes time paid for by the people of the State—not to mention expenses—we see the example set which each one of the 6000 employees whom he directs is expected to follow.

That is what this monstrous political machine was created for and that is what it does.

And never in what were heretofore the worst days of this boss-ridden State was there ever a political machine so minute in its ramifications, so unscrupulous in its methods, so malignant in its attacks on honest men, so reckless in its procedure, so costly to the people, so ruthless in its persecutions, so hateful in its spirit or so destructive in its effects."

What had the Progressives accomplished in their first term?

_____

Evaluate the arguments against Johnson in 1910 and 1914.

_____

Based on the newspaper record here, why did both the Republican and Democratic parties field candidates in 1914?

_____

Optional Exercise

TO GO DEEPER:

Research and write a paper on the impact of Hiram Johnson and the Progressives on the structure of party politics in California. Be certain to consult George Mowry, *The California Progressives* (Berkeley: University of California Press, 1951); Spencer Olin, Jr., *California's Prodigal Sons: Hiram Johnson and the Progressives, 1911–1917* (Berkeley: University of California Press, 1968); Kevin Starr, *Inventing the Dream: California Through the Progressive Era* (New York: Oxford University Press, 1985); William Deverell and Tom Sitton, eds., *California Progressivism Revisited* (Berkeley: University of California Press, 1994); and Jackson K. Putnam, "The Pattern of Modern California Politics," *Pacific Historical Review* 61 (February, 1992), pp. 23–52.

Name_____   Instructor_____   Date_____

Exercise 7

Read the following documents and consider the 1958 election as a pivotal event in modern California politics.

1. *Los Angeles Times,* September 18, 1957
     "[Governor Goodwin] Knight said he has not "given any thought" to whether he will support Nixon or [U.S. Senator William] Knowland for the GOP Presidential nomination in 1960. Asked if he stands by his earlier accusation that Knowland seeks to use the Governorship as a "stepping stone" to the Presidency, he replied:
     "I made the statement before. I haven't given it any thought this morning."
     The Governor explained that his original purpose in coming to Washington was to discuss the California political situation with [Richard M.] Nixon. He said the visit with President Eisenhower evolved from a discussion with Presidential Assistant Sherman Adams when Adams made a speech in San Francisco last month. Knight said he would like to discuss the California scene with the President, and the appointment was arranged."

2. *Los Angeles Times,* October 4, 1957
     "Sen. Knowland officially announced his candidacy for the Governorship of California today and Gov. Knight, the man he hopes to unseat, denounced the decision "as a hydra-headed bid for the Presidency.""

3. *Los Angeles Times,* November 6, 1957
     "Gov. Knight today announced his withdrawal as a candidate for the Governorship to run for the Senate next year.
     Knight's announcement followed a visit to President Eisenhower and a visit to Vice-President Nixon.
     'The decision is my own,' he declared."

4. Stewart Alsop, "The Great California Drama," *Saturday Evening Post,* October 18, 1958:
     The 1958 campaign "intimately involves the fate of three major aspirants to the Presidency of these United States. It will profoundly affect the internal coloration of both major parties. It will have a powerful impact on American foreign policy. It will determine, perhaps for years to come, the political control of what will soon be our biggest state. Perhaps above all, it will go a long way toward establishing whether the Republican Party is destined to permanent minority status in the nation."

5. *Sacramento Bee,* November 5, 1958
                    Brown's Victory is Growing: Engle and Mosk Sweep In
     "A smashing victory for Attorney General Edmund G. (Pat) Brown, rolling steadily toward landslide proportions, today gave the Democrats their first California governorship in 20 years, their second in the century.
     Brown tore his Republican opponent, United States Senator William F. Knowland to shreds in yesterday's election and eliminated the senate minority leader from political life."

Considering the evidence in the primary sources in this section, to what degree do national influences impact California Republican politics?

Name   Instructor   Date

Write a paper on why the 1958 election could be considered significant in California and national politics. Remember the words of Stewart Alsop and consider what the California legislature under Brown produced in the four years that followed, what happened in national politics in the 1960 election, and the direction of national public policy and foreign relations. Be certain to consult Jacqueline R. Braitman, "Elizabeth Snyder and the Role of Women in the Postwar Resurgence of California's Democratic Party," *Pacific Historical Review* 62 (May, 1992), pp. 197–220, and Kurt R. Schuparra, "Freedom versus Tyranny: The 1958 California Election and the Origin of the State's Conservative Movement," *Pacific Historical Review* 63 (November, 1994), pp. 537–560.

Name   Instructor   Date